Holy Ground:
Have You Been There?

By Connie Wohlford

Holy Ground: Have You Been There?

Preface

Holy Ground: Have You Been There? is basically an anthology—a collection of stories, yet not ordinary stories. These are true stories from the lives of real people in which the individuals have each had a supernatural encounter with God, Holy Spirit, Jesus, or an angel sent by God. Some of the encounters are the accounts of events of people in the Bible. Others are experiences—testimonies—of modern-day ordinary folks personally known by the author.

Each of the forty stories tells of a supernatural encounter that was life-changing for that individual. These are holy moments in which the person found themselves on holy ground with a holy presence, never to be the same afterwards. In most instances the trajectory of their lives was reversed or greatly altered from that moment on.

Hopefully, the reader will be encouraged in their faith in Creator God, discovering or affirming that God is all powerful, supernatural, and desires good for all Mankind. Also, it is desired that people will see that God still does supernatural works in the lives of people today. Many of these encounters seem otherworldly—yes. That's because they are.

"And they overcame him by the blood of the Lamb, and by the word of their testimony" (Revelation 12:11 KJV).

Dedication

I would like to dedicate my book, *Holy Ground: Have You Been There?* to the Holy Spirit, the third Person of the Trinity. The true stories recorded in this book were orchestrated by Him. I hope the reader will see His presence in each of these stories as He reveals His nature as the Comforter, the Helper, the Paraclete, the Presence of God, the Spirit of Truth, the Healer, the Baptizer, the Counselor, the Advocate, the Spirit of Holiness, the Strengthener, the Spirit of Mercy, the Spirit of Life, the Spirit of Grace, the Breath of God. We could go on. He is everything we need for life and godliness. (2 Peter: 1:3). In this book, He is the main Character and the Hero.

Also, I am dedicating *Holy Ground: Have You Been There?* to Charlie Maney and his dear wife Betty Jo Maney. The Lord sent this precious couple into my family's life at a time when I was spiritually hungry and thirsty just as the dear pants for the water brook, in Psalm 42:1. In my heart I knew there was more to God and more to serving Him than I had learned in my thirty years of Sunday School and church attendance. From Charlie and Betty Jo, I learned about the ways in which the Holy Spirit is directly involved in the lives of people today—every day.

Thank You, Abba Father, for sending Him—the Promise of the Father—to benefit us in so many ways. And thank You for sending Charlie and Betty Jo to our family in the 1980s. We're forever grateful.

So, in the name of Jesus and for His glory, I dedicate this book, *Holy Ground: Have You Been There?*

Connie Wohlford

Introduction

"In Heaven You will be with God but on earth He will be with you." Anonymous

This book, *Holy Ground: Have You Been There?* shares forty true stories from real people. Some of the stories tell of situations of individuals in the Bible, including the Old Testament and the New Testament. Also, many of the stories are instances where modern day individuals, men and women known personally by the author, have had supernatural encounters which were life-changing experiences.

While reading these accounts, the reader is invited to consider why God chose this person for their unique encounter and/or task. Also, though not all asked for it or expected it, how did each individual prepare themselves for the encounter and what was the result of each one?

Many will say that as believers and followers of Christ Jesus we continuously are on holy ground because the Holy Spirit dwells inside us. That's certainly true, but this book focuses on noteworthy occasions when the individuals are intensely aware of God's holy presence on holy ground for a holy life-altering purpose.

I have walked with my Savior, Jesus Christ, for many years. I admit, I've had my share of failures, but there have been occasions when I have stepped right into the Holy of Holies, or I could say that the Holy of Holies has overtaken me. That is certainly Holy Ground.

My friend, J. D. Wininger, says, "It's in the fertile soil of your soul that God can produce the greatest harvest." Let's each one open our soul and spirit to our Creator and allow Him to transform it into fertile Holy Ground for His use that will produce a great harvest in the building of His Eternal Kingdom.

Be blessed and encouraged as you read the testimonies recorded in this book. Our Heavenly Father desires to intimately lead each of us and walk with us every minute of every day. "The LORD thy God in the midst of thee is mighty; he will save, he will rejoice over thee with joy; he will rest in his love, he will joy over thee with singing" (Zephaniah 3:17 KJV).

It is my prayer that as you read these pages you will find yourself on holy ground in awe of the amazing things our God has done. Allow Abba Father to minister life, hope, and peace to you in whatever situation you are currently experiencing.

You will notice that at the end of each story the reader is invited to share thoughts, comments, and prayer requests on social media using the hashtag, #HolyGroundAndMe. Do join in the conversation if you'd like.

May God's richest blessings overtake you. Connie Wohlford

"And they overcame him by the blood of the Lamb, and by the word of their testimony" *(Revelation 12:11a KJV)*

Table Of Contents

Table Of Contents

The Wind
(Connie Wohlford)

"Lord, this is wonderful, but I don't think I can stand it any longer. If You don't stop, I'm going to end up on the floor. What will everyone think?"

Those were my words, spoken from my spirit to God. Oh, how I have regretted resisting the supernatural move of God in my life that day. Has He moved in my life supernaturally since then? Yes, many times, but not in the same way.

Nothing like that had ever happened to me before and I was unfamiliar with such things. In our rather normal mainline church manifestations of God's presence had not been seen, at least, not by me. But I had been searching—yearning—for more of God. I was so hungry for the things of God and He knew it.

That Sunday morning after hearing a message from a lay-preacher friend, my husband, our two elementary school aged sons, and I stood, singing the closing hymn of the service. Then it happened.

From the upper right-hand corner of the vaulted ceiling of the sanctuary it came. I heard it. It grew louder and louder as it came down directly onto me. No other sounds entered my ears.

I knew exactly what it was because I had read about it in my Bible. It was *the mighty rushing wind*, spoken of in Acts 2:2, and it was from God just for me. Its roar was violent and loud as it wrapped around me like a cocoon, and it was wonderful. As it swirled around me, I knew I was in God's presence and in His care. Though it seemed like minutes, I suppose it took no time at all. I thought I might fall to the floor under its power, but I knew I wouldn't get hurt.

My mind said: *What if I fall down. What would my family think was happening to me? What would everyone in the church think if I ended up on the floor. Oh God, if this keeps up, I'm going to fall. You have to stop.* In my thoughts, I repeated those words.

So then, the wind began to rescind. Slowly that wonderful cocoon unwrapped from my body and the incredible wind began to retract upward, gradually getting softer and softer until it went back through the same upper righthand corner of the ceiling from whence it came. It was gone and I was left standing there with my family. We turned and exited the pew just like we always did.

I didn't tell anyone until years later. How could I find the words to explain such an experience? No one would understand. But I was never the same again. I had been in a holy place—on holy ground—with my Heavenly Father. Though I was already born-again, through that experience I was born afresh. I had been washed anew with living water and anointed with the oil of the Holy Spirit. The fire of the Holy Ghost filled my spirit.

I did not speak in tongues that day and if I had, I would have been clueless about what was happening. Though born and raised in an evangelical church, I'd never heard of such things. If I had not asked God to stop, I believe I would have ended up on the floor and would have spoken in a holy language unfamiliar to all around me.

I do still regret not allowing God to finish whatever work He wanted for me that day. I wish that my fear of man had not taken over the moment. Nonetheless, it had a mighty positive impact on me in powerful ways. I received indisputable assurance of my salvation, plus the undeniable reality that my Heavenly Father wants to move in my life. He sees me. He knows me. He loves me. God continues hewing and growing me and the more I cooperate with Him, the more He accomplishes in and through me.

"And suddenly there came a sound from heaven, as of a rushing mighty wind, and it filled the whole house where they were sitting" (Acts 2:2).

Let's pray: *Holy Father, thank You for giving us tastes and glimpses of the wonder of You. Thank You for surprising us with Your holy presence, even when we're not expecting it. What a mighty God You are! Help us to welcome Your supernatural works and not be embarrassed or hesitant to enjoy and be ministered to by them. We know that all You do is for our good. Thank You, Lord. In Jesus' name we pray, amen.*

I have never heard anyone else talk about hearing and being wrapped up in God's mighty rushing wind though I suspect it has happened to others. If you or someone you know has had a similar experience, please let us know, using the hashtag, #HolyGroundAndMe, on your social media platforms. We can encourage one another with our testimonies.

A Consequential Call
(Abram/Abraham – Old Testament)

Then it happened—a holy moment and Abram was listening.

"Now the LORD said to Abram: 'Get out of your country ... to a land I will show you. I will make you a great nation; I will bless you and make your name great; and you shall be a blessing. I will bless those who bless you, and I will curse him who curses you; and in you all the families of the earth shall be blessed'" (Genesis 12:1-3).

Thus, the Jewish nation was born.

Abram heard God's voice and said, "Yes," to the call of Yahweh—a call more consequential than he could have imagined. Then, when the time was right, God changed his name to Abraham.

Abram left his father and the comfort of the heritage he knew. He took his wife, Sarai, whose name was later changed to Sarah. Also with him were his nephew, Lot, and a few others. He took livestock, tents, and provisions and set out to Canaan under God's instructions. He was seventy-five years old at the time and childless.

But he believed God. In that holy moment he knew he was on holy ground and that the God of the universe was speaking to him. That holy visitation was not simply life-changing for Abram and his family. It literally impacted the trajectory of Mankind.

When the time was right, through God's miracles, the barren elderly Sarah gave birth to Isaac, who later fathered Jacob. During a wrestling match with the Angel of the Lord, God changed Jacob's name to Israel. We may read that interesting account in the thirty second chapter of Genesis. The twelve sons of Israel/Jacob were Reuben, Simeon, Levi, Judah, Dan, Naphtali, Gad, Asher, Issachar, Zebulun, Joseph, and Benjamin. There we have the twelve tribes of Israel.

God had now set His redemption plan in motion. In the fullness of time, according to Father God's clock, He visited the simple Jewish teenager, Mary, and Redemption was born and placed in a feeding trough in Bethlehem. His Hebrew name is Yeshuah. We call

Him, Jesus. He is Son of God, Son of Man.

Let's pray: *Holy Father, as we consider Your calling on Abraham help us to know that You have had an amazing plan for Mankind from the beginning of Creation. Help me to be assured that I am part of that plan. Thank You, Lord. And help me to never forget that the Jewish people were set apart by You to bring redemption through Your Son, Jesus—Yeshua. It's in His wonderful name we pray, amen.*

Have you had a visitation from your Creator—a holy moment—when God spoke something consequential to you? Was it an impression in your spirit, through a Scripture Passage, or even the audible voice of God? Did it cause a course correction, a relocation, or greatly changed your mind or even the direction of your life? If so, please share your experience on social media using the hashtag #HolyGroundAndMe

An Unexpected Visitation
(Zacharias – Old Testament)

"What's taking him so long?" the people were asking as they waited outside the Temple.

Never before had it taken so much time for a priest to perform the task of burning incense in the Holy Place. Twice daily, morning and evening, the high priest administered this ritual according to the Law. But today was a special day—a most holy day—observed only once a year. It was Yom Kipper, the Day of Atonement, the most solemn of Jewish holidays. On this day Jews seek expiation of their sins and a fresh start with a clean slate.

Since it was a once in a lifetime privilege, maybe the high priest, Zacharias, was lingering to enjoy the experience. But, no, that would be deemed a prideful act, and this holy man wouldn't dare do such a thing. Entering into the sacred area of the Temple was much too solemn and Zacharias was known to be righteous before God.

He was taking care of business just as required, but an unexpected delay occurred. A sudden interruption which would change his life, as well as the course of the world, had happened.

Suddenly, to the right of the altar of incense, stood the angel, Gabriel, and Zacharias was filled with fear at the sight.

"But the angel said to him, 'Do not be afraid, Zacharias, for your prayer is heard; and your wife Elizabeth will bear you a son, and you shall call his name John'" (Luke 1:13).

Zacharias found himself, not just in a holy place on holy ground, but in a holy moment in the presence of a holy angel, delivering a personal message just for him. The sight of the angel struck him with fear and the message he carried was beyond belief.

In fact, Zacharias initially did not believe the message because he and Elizabeth were both advanced in age and well beyond becoming parents. For decades they had hoped for a child. Because of his unbelief, Gabriel told him that he would be mute, unable to talk until the promise had been fulfilled. And it was so.

On the day when their new baby's name was to be announced Zacharias' tongue was loosed and he proclaimed that his son's name was John. Onlookers were surprised because by tradition a family name was used, and this was not a family name. But Zacharias had met with God's messenger and knew that God had ordained that the name should be John and so it was.

Zacharias would always remember that amazing encounter on the Day of Atonement. He realized that his son would be special in God's eyes but probably could not have imagined the significance of the ministry of John the Baptist, the forerunner of Jesus the Christ. He would be the very one described as, ***"The voice of one crying in the wilderness, 'Prepare ye the way of the Lord, make his paths straight'"*** (Mark 1:3 KJV).

In the next few verses of the first chapter of Luke, Gabriel gives Zacharias more details about the coming birth of this John. It's a beautiful story and I encourage you to go read it.

Let's pray: *Holy Father, what an awesome God You are. Thank You for sending John the Baptist to help prepare the way for Jesus' incarnation. Your plan and Your ways are so amazing, and Your involvement of ordinary people is incredible. Thank You for ministering angels who do Your bidding. We glorify You, Holy One, and thank You for all You do for our benefit. In Jesus' name we pray, amen.*

Have you had a visitation from an angel—a holy moment—when God sent His messenger to comfort you or tell you something important? If so, please share your experience on social media using the hashtag #HolyGroundAndMe

God Knows Best
(Suzie)

When my husband, Greg and I were first married, I was a new Christian. I was full of zeal and very dedicated to my church. As would be expected, I wanted my husband to attend church with me and it truly bothered me that he wasn't on board. I continued to pray for him and, although I knew he loved me very much, I couldn't convince him to attend church with me.

Greg had a good foundation; unlike me he had been brought up in a Christian home. I knew he feared God, but he just wasn't ready to commit to God and regular church attendance.

Almost five years later, my sister invited us to visit at her church. My husband thought it was a good idea, and we went. The next week he mentioned wanting to go back. I was reluctant, because I was very comfortable at my own church and struggled with what people would think if I stopped going there. I battled with whether this was the Lord's will or not.

I agreed to go back to this church and after a few times of visiting, my husband raised his hand to rededicate his life to the Lord. As one of the men from the church came and prayed with Greg, I began to cry and to thank God.

At that moment, the Lord spoke to me. I knew I was hearing God's voice, though not audibly. I felt as though I was immersed in the presence of God. Indeed, I was standing on holy ground.

He clearly told me that I needed to keep my eyes on Him, and He would take care of Greg. In that holy moment I received clarity and peace in my spirit because I understood that God was at work in my husband. It was not my responsibility to grow Greg spiritually. It was God's responsibility, and He was well able to handle it.

This experience changed my life and made a huge difference in how I related to my husband and how I related to God. It made me realize each person's relationship with God is personal between them and God. I also realized that God had heard my prayers, but that He would answer on His terms and His timetable. What a relief to be able to turn Greg over to God. It had been too much for me to carry myself.

We can always be sure that God knows better than we in every life situation.

"For my thoughts are not your thoughts, neither are your ways my ways, saith the LORD. For as the heavens are higher than the earth, so are my ways higher than your ways, and my thoughts than your thoughts" (Isaiah 55:8-9 KJV).

"And we know that all things work together for good to them that love God, to them who are the called according to his purpose" (Romans 8:28 KJV).

What a difference it makes when we give God the things that trouble us. I Peter 5:7 tells us to cast our cares onto God and even tells us why. It's because He cares for us. Anything that concerns us, in turn, concerns our Heavenly Father.

Let's pray: *Oh Father, I'm so grateful that You care about things that I care about. AND, You know what's best in every situation and how to best handle every situation. Thank You, Lord. Please help me to learn to care more about the things that You care about. In Jesus' name I pray, amen.*

Are you carrying a burden or concern that you should turn over to God? Or have you experienced the relief of casting your cares onto Him? Please tell us about it, using the hashtag #HolyGroundAndMe

Come In
(Jesus – New Testament)

It was the ninth hour of the day. The sky had darkened even though it was midday.

Jesus cried out, ***"'It is finished:' and he bowed his head, gave up the ghost"*** (John 19:30b KJV).

The crowd that mocked and the few who mourned stumbled as the earth shook.

"Then behold, the veil of the temple was rent in twain from the top to the bottom; and the earth did quake, and the rocks rent" (Matthew 27:51 KJV).

Why was the veil of the temple torn in two and, notably, from top to bottom? Understanding the purpose of the veil gives understanding of the great significance of the veil being torn. It had never happened before and was alarming to all who were aware of the occurrence.

We learn about God's instructions regarding the veil in Exodus 26. It hung in the temple separating the Most Holy Place,–the Holy of Holies,—from the Holy Place. The only physical item in the Holy of Holies was the Ark of the Covenant and more importantly there resided the presence of God. Only the high priest was allowed to enter and that would happen once a year, on the Day of Atonement.

[Side Note: *Atonement* means "expiation, reconciliation." *Expiation* means the removal of guilt through the payment of a penalty. *]

Jesus' death on the cross atoned for the sin of Mankind and opened the way for us to have full access to Father God—Adonai—our Lord God, Master, and Creator. We may call Him *Abba*, like saying *Daddy*.

Human hands could not have torn that thick and durable veil, especially from the top. It was thirty feet high and three and a half to four inches thick.

From above, God Himself ripped the veil, as if to say, "Your sin penalty has been paid in full. My only Son has become the spotless sacrificial Lamb and His blood has been applied on the altar. He has been slain to atone for all your sins and you have been washed clean. Now, come in and abide with Me. Walk with Me. Fellowship with Me. Believe in My Son, and His once for all payment made for you, and be saved. This is My love gift to whosoever will receive it."

John the Baptist had prophesied of Jesus' atoning sacrifice when he saw Him walking toward him and said, ***"Behold! The Lamb of God who takes away the sin of the world!"*** (John 1:29b).

So … God has made a way for us to enter the Holy of Holies and be in His presence, the place where He dwells. Once we believe and receive Christ Jesus as our personal Savior, His Spirit dwells in us permanently.

If you are a born-again follower of Christ Jesus, likely you have sensed the presence of God in your own walk. When we read and meditate on Scripture and when we pray, we set ourselves up for having holy encounters with our Heavenly Father through His Spirit.

Let's pray: *Holy Father, we are humbled to think that You want to have fellowship with us—that You, Creator of the universe, desire for each of us to be in Your family and in Your Eternal Kingdom. Oh God, we're so grateful! Thank You for sending Jesus to earth to become the sacrificial Lamb, pouring out His blood to redeem us from the clutches of sin and give us access to You—to go behind the veil and live in Your holy presence, walking and talking, and being Your own. In the wonderful name of Jesus, we pray—amen.*

Please share your experiences using this hashtag on social media platforms: #HolyGroundAndMe.

*The Hebrew-Greek Key Word Study Bible, 2008 by AMG International, Inc., Chattanooga, TN, page 1712

A Miracle!
(James Rathman)

Having had two heart attacks, two days apart, eleven heart procedures, five stents, and seven heart strength tests of 14% to 20%, I was assigned to cardiologists who treat patients who were nearing death. In the midst of this, five people who did not know one another contacted me, and told me that the Holy Spirit told them I needed to switch cardiologists, and some said that their message from the Holy Spirit included, that if I did not, I would pass away! None of these people knew I was already considering switching cardiologists. I already had concerns about passing away and one of my cardiologists had stated that without a heart transplant, I would die.

Later, in November 2021, I was completing the last of the physical tests needed, to get on a heart transplant list at a heart transplant center. As a well-known and respected heart transplant cardiologist inserted a catheter into an artery in my neck I asked, "About how long do I have to live with my heart like this?" He replied, "About two years." Then he added, trying to comfort and encourage me, "But don't worry—that's why we're doing this. We are trying to help you."

I realized that without a heart transplant, I had until about November 2023 to live. In that same time-period, in 2021, a Christian friend, named Amy, who had exceeding resolve in life, and a wonderful faith and love for Jesus, called me. With the Holy Spirit speaking through her, Amy told me that I would pass away in October 2023 if I did not get a heart transplant.

I was only going to listen to the message from the Holy Spirit coming through Amy, including such precise timing that I would die in the month of October 2023, without a heart transplant. I found it interesting that the cardiologist had stated that at about the same time, I would die.

During that same time frame, I had a liver biopsy in order to qualify for the heart transplant list. One week later, I collapsed at home, unconscious from liver bleeding, and woke up only by the grace of Jesus and called 911. I ended up in a hospital ICU unit, and then another unit for six days. My liver had been accidentally pierced during the biopsy at the heart transplant center. A surgeon told me that I was going to die because it was too precarious for me to be transported an hour away to the heart transplant center which also specialized in the liver.

Jesus was clearly with me. Having defied the surgeon's diagnosis about dying from the liver issue, I gained strength and left the hospital. After going through such an extensive process, I still could not get on the transplant list due to a technicality. I could not fill the center's requirement of having a caregiver within a certain radius of the heart transplant center, who could stay next to me for twenty-four hours a day, for ninety days, after the transplant. I only knew of a few people in that area, and they either had families to care for or had jobs. I did not realize it at the time, but this turned out to be a blessing. I knew I had to be obedient to the Holy Spirit and get a heart transplant. However, I kept praying and hoping that Jesus would heal my heart.

One day, I could sense in the Holy Spirit, that I was to give a testimony about different aspects of healing, and when needed, help others. This included that God approves of medical science treatment, and medications. And of course, Jesus heals directly at any time He desires, including through prayer. I also sensed in the Holy Spirit, that at times, God will guide in a combination of these ways for healing. The Holy Spirit also told me to testify that God's children are to eat healthy natural foods for the body He gave us, which is a Temple of the Holy Spirit.

In the early Spring 2023, while walking near a lake I passed by a woman in a parked car. She said hello, and asked if I wanted prayer. I explained my health situation to her and specifically requested, "Don't pray for healing, though, pray for a successful heart transplant only because that was what Jesus wanted me to do!" She prayed, and the Holy Spirit poured upon us in a beautiful manifestation! I learned that her name was Melissa, and I refrained from telling her—to not make her self-conscience—that she was, lit up, as a bright light in the Spirit of Holy Jesus by the end of the prayer!

Not long after that, a friend, a servant of Jesus named Susan, called me. In addition to her regular job, for over twenty years she specialized in volunteering and helping those in need. She told me that she had a prior vision from God and was not allowed to tell me until right then. Susan said that she had a vision of a Bible story— Abraham, who was ready to sacrifice his son, Isaac, and the Angel of God told him to pull back at the last moment!

Susan told me that she sensed in the Holy Spirit, that God was eliminating the need for the heart transplant, and that He would heal me before I would die in October of 2023! I was thinking through this incredible message while on the phone with her … and then it happened. Suddenly, I was enlightened! I told Susan how this was pieced together. I was resigned to having complete obedience to God to get the heart transplant when I asked the woman, Melissa, to pray at the lake. Jesus was apparently rewarding my obedience.

After I got off the phone with Susan, I could not fully grasp the message and its magnitude. The enormity of the love of Jesus was beyond comprehension! I had denied Jesus for decades and He still had such grace and mercy on me! I did not even know how to praise Him enough!

My friend Susan was tone deaf as a child and was informed by a singing coach that she would never sing well. She prayed for a singing voice, and Jesus gave her one that matured over the years. Her voice had grown into a beautiful opera, singing prayers in the Holy Spirit for healing. At the Holy Spirit's guidance, Susan sang on the phone to me for two months, about three minutes a day for sixty-two days straight. She was singing opera prayers for healing through the Holy Spirit.

Each day Susan sang over the phone, and I did not want it to end! Each day as she sang, I felt powerful and varying levels of euphoric closeness to the Holy Spirit! Within the beautiful manifestations of the Holy Spirit as Susan sang, I sought new ways to praise Jesus, including giving thanks in my mind of praise to Him! These were like holy moments in the presence of Holy Spirit on holy ground. No words are sufficient to describe it.

During this time-period, I was also guided to read God's Word for healing, and dear friends and strangers were also praying for my healing. This included an incredible experience after a church service, with endearing friends. A wonderful Christian couple, named Michael and Pamela, gathered the church's prayer group. The Holy Spirit poured upon us as they prayed. Then, complete strangers were taking turns speaking to me with such moving Christ-like love—words with wonderful and loving encouragement of hope and faith-building. I struggled to hold back tears. It took me three days to process the experience—such a beautiful manifestation of the Holy Spirit and feeling so cared for from those who were mostly strangers!

Prior to those two months of the healing opera prayers from Susan, I was out of breath, exhausted upon standing, lightheaded, was getting weaker. My body was noticeably deteriorating and dying. I was bed bound about four to five days out of the week for twenty-three hours each day. Even before the two months of the healing opera prayer was completed, I began to have strength I had not had in years. Toward the end, and right after the sixty-two days of prayer for healing, I was increasingly walking and jogging for over a mile and a half, running wind sprints, doing fifteen to twenty-five reps of dips, and approximately fifty, half push-ups, in one set. By then, it was August of 2023, just two months before I was previously set to pass away, and I was elatedly praising Jesus as never before!

Also, during those two months, at a revival, a wonderful Spirit-filled man of great faith, named Edwin, prayed healing over me, and I felt an immediate and noticeable improvement to my health! Jesus clearly intervened and healed my heart during those months! I could breathe as I had not been able to for years, and I was moving forward in an exciting new season to witness, serve, and testify of our Lord and Savior, JESUS, WHO IS LOVE!

One day, an extraordinary Christian named Rena, a woman of a bright light, love, faith, and heartfelt passion to serve Jesus, was sitting to my right. She suddenly placed her left hand on my chest. Rena looked at me and exclaimed, "Jesus really *did* heal your heart!!!" She explained, that right before she placed her hand on my chest, she had a vision of a red healthy heart with a healthy blue vein running through the heart, and she understood that Jesus had healed me.

This was an extraordinary experience, for many reasons! I knew

I would *not only* never forget this blessing from Jesus, and that moment with Rena, a Holy Spirit messenger…but I also believed that through the rest of my life I would keep trying to fully embrace the magnitude of the blessing and the logistics of it!

I later prayed and considered having new heart tests done but Jesus had given me abundant proof of my heart being healed by Him. This included having been mostly bed bound, and then being up, running sprints, and conducting other exercises and activities which would not have been possible for someone with my previous heart condition. I had also received the message from the Holy Spirit through Rena of a healthy heart.

Very shortly after the healing, I sensed in the Holy Spirit I was to be bold and spread the testimony of how Jesus healed my heart, for hope and faith-building to help others.

In the midst of this healing, the generous Spirit of Holy Jesus sent an additional blessing that changed my life into a type of joy I had never felt! Thanks to Jesus, I'm awake late at night at times, not from suffering, but literally from having met so much joy in my life that I cannot sleep! There is too much to testify of and too much to praise Jesus for to not storm castles praising the gift of life and God's Glory of love in Jesus! I am overcome with ***"joy unspeakable and full of glory"*** (1 Peter 1:8b KJV). My newfound joy declares how can we all not seek new ways to give great praise to Jesus, and to testify to others who need hope and or salvation of eternal life and eternal love through Jesus Christ!

Rejoice with me in the truth of Isaiah 53:5. ***"But he was wounded for our transgressions, he was bruised for our iniquities: the chastisement of our peace was upon him; and with his stripes we are healed"*** (KJV). Thank You, Jesus!

Let's pray: *Oh Father, thank You for love and Your great healing power. Help us to always seek You when we're in need and trust You. We're so grateful for Your answers to our prayers and we praise and glorify Your holy name. And it's in that wonderful name of Jesus, we pray, amen.*

Lived & written in August of 2024 by James Rathman, Deliverance Ministry. ~~~ Evangelist: BlessedInternational.com; Correspondence: OneLostsheepMinistry33@Gmail.com

Has the Lord healed you of a physical illness? Are you in need of healing and would like for us to pray for you? Please comment using the hashtag, #HolyGroundAndMe

I AM and I Will
(Moses – Old Testament)

Wanted for murder, he would never go back to Egypt again—at least that's what he thought. Two hundred fifty miles should be plenty of desert between his old life and his new life with his new family and new job.

But then it happened.

While tending his father-in-law's flock Moses was captivated by the strangest sight he'd ever beheld. A bush was on fire, but it was not being consumed. How do the leaves on a bush remain whole and green while the bush continues in flames?

The phenomenon had this stunned man's full attention.

Then an even greater marvel—the voice of God Himself came from the bush. The Book of Exodus describes it like this:

"And the Angel of the LORD appeared to him in a flame of fire from the midst of a bush. So he looked, and behold, the bush was burning with fire, but the bush was not consumed. Then Moses said, 'I will now turn aside to see this great sight, why the bush does not burn.'

"So when the Lord saw that he turned aside to look, God called to him from the midst of the bush and said, 'Moses, Moses!' And he said, 'Here I am.'

"Then He said, 'Do not draw near this place. Take your sandals off your feet, for the place where you stand is holy ground.' Moreover He said, 'I am the God of your father—the God of Abraham, the God of Isaac, and the God of Jacob.' And Moses hid his face, for he was afraid to look upon God" (Exodus 3:2-6).

Having Moses' full attention, God disclosed His great plan to bring the Israelites out of bondage in Egypt, and God had chosen Moses to lead the great exodus. Though he grew up in the palace of Egypt, Moses had become a fugitive and a common shepherd for livestock which he didn't even own himself. After a bit of resistance and uncertainty Moses began to yield when God said, *"I will certainly be with you"* (Exodus 3:12a).

With that assurance, God gave Moses more insight into His plan. But knowing he had no standing with the people of his birth, Moses continued to question God and stated that he didn't even know what to call this amazing God.

"And God said to Moses, 'I AM WHO I AM.' And He said, 'Thus you shall say to the children of Israel, "I AM has sent me to you"' (Exodus 3:14).

After further instructions, Moses was convinced that God had called him, would be with him, and would show him the way. We can say, "The rest is history."

Side Note: If you have never read it or it's been a while, I recommend that you read the next few chapters in the Book of Exodus and see how God miraculously delivered His people from the brutal jaws of Egypt.

Moses' unexpected holy moment on holy ground changed the trajectory of his and his people's lives. Even greater, the trajectory of the human race was altered. God's chosen people were delivered from slavery in Egypt, were given the Ten Commandments, and established a homeland, Israel. Under God's mighty hand our Creator paved the way and set up the place where approximately 1,750 years later Jesus would be born in a manger.

The same God who visited Moses; the same God who called Moses; the same God who said to Moses, *"I will certainly be with you,"* is the same God who has visited us, called us, and said He will certainly be with us.

This is our time in history. It's our time to turn our face toward God, give Him our full attention, listen to His instructions, and follow the path He directs us onto.

We may not lead a nation from captivity, but we may lead a person out of slavery to sin through the shed blood of Jesus Christ and show them the way into the hope of Eternal Life.

Let's pray: *Holy Father, we're in awe of the way You called and led Moses and the Israelites. Thank You for doing that as You prepared the way for Jesus to come to earth and provide us with an exodus out of the slavery of sin. Help me now, Lord, to walk in Your ways and fulfil the call You have for me. In Jesus' name I pray, amen.*

Have you encountered God in a burning bush kind of moment? Have you turned your face toward the God of Moses? If so, please tell us about it using the hashtag, #HolyGroundAndMe

Encounter with Spirit Armies
(Donna Hankla)

I lived in a room with two other girls at Emory & Henry College, Emory, Viriginia. We each shared a deep belief in the power of prayer, and we attended Bible Study groups.

After supper, one autumn evening, I was delighted to feel refreshing bursts of wind blowing into the room from an open window. Soon, the evening would turn into the dark of the night. I took a break from exhausting study sessions for an anatomy test the following day. I looked out the window and saw vibrant colors of fall all around us. The college campus was surrounded by hills which were dotted with numerous trees. The leaves had turned into brilliant colors of yellow and red.

Soon, I laid down and dozed off to sleep. My eyes had become heavy with sleep. But I would not sleep very long. A luminous light lit up the entire room. The light switch was turned off! The other girls sat up in their beds. We realized that God's presence was in our midst, so we began to pray. After about an hour, it became evident that this would be an all-night visit.

We sensed in our spirits that we should stay awake and pray and wait in the presence of the Lord. We all knew that we should stay alert. We were about to experience an encounter that would last a lifetime. For indeed, one of the girls became a Methodist minister. I obtained bachelor's and master's degrees in education. Also, I became an ordained minister, and a prayer leader.

Suddenly, I heard LOUD marching. It was so loud that I was drawn to the window to see what was happening. I thought that the cadets were practicing. There was a Marching Army, but it was not of this world. Angelic beings were marching! I could tell that they were following a Spirit General. They marched right by my window. They marched in a cadence. Angel after angel just kept coming. It seemed that they marched for at least 30 minutes!

I wanted to know what was happening. So, I asked the Lord about this marching army.

And I sensed that the Holy Spirit gave the following response:

"This is the army of the Lord. You will join this army in due time. It will be an army of intercessors. You will meet many prayer warriors."

"They shall run like mighty men; they shall climb the wall like men of war; and they shall march every one on his ways, and they shall not break their ranks" (Joel 2:7 KJV).

Shortly after midnight, we all fell asleep. But we would not sleep long. This was a night for us to wait in God's presence. And God's Spirit would help us keep this Prayer Watch!

The room began to shake so violently that the beds literally moved a few feet! No sleep for us. This heavenly encounter was of greater value than sleep! It was a supernatural holy thing, and I was changed.

After this encounter with the Marching Spirits, I became more zealous to pursue a life of prayer and became a leader of prayer on several different levels. Without doubting, I knew God had called me to a life of intercessory prayer and to encourage others to pray as well and I'll never forget it.

Are you a person of prayer? Many Christians don't seem to realize the importance of and the power in a life of prayer. I'm sure the Bible tells us to pray without ceasing for a reason, in 1 Thessalonians 5:16.

Let's pray: *Oh God, from Your Word, we know that You want us to pray. You've stated it many times and in many ways. Help me to grasp the value of prayer and to desire to meet with You in that holy experience. I don't need an army of angels to confirm this to me but thank You for showing Donna this incredible sight and if You decide to send an angel to show me something I welcome that. Thank You for Your great love for me. In Jesus' name I pray, amen.*

Have you had a visitation of angels? If so, how did it affect you? Also, how's your prayer life? If so, please share your experience on social media using the hashtag, #HolyGroundAndMe

Side Note: A friend asked me (Connie) that question, "How's your prayer life?" many years ago. We had been discussing a certain big life problem I was experiencing. That question really struck a chord with me, and I pondered it and talked to God about it. I realized I needed to pray more. So, I picked up the pace and soon realized it was bringing me into a closer walk with my Savior. Plus, God did answer that prayer request regarding my situation.

More information about Author, Donna Hankla:

With great joy Mary Donna Hankla shares encounters with God that inspired her to become an intercessor for the nation. At the age of 17, she began experiencing prophetic words and scenes from the Holy Spirit. Every experience has been confirmed by the golden standard, God's Word!

The fight for her family was the first heavenly order. Her family instilled values of diligence, dedication, and hard work. Many summers were spent working on the farm, tending crops such as tobacco, beans, strawberries, and squash. These crops provided money for her college education. The entire family believed in the importance of good jobs.

However, the family experienced great struggles during her teenage years. These struggles brought Donna to Bible Study groups held before the start of school. God's Spirit moved powerfully during the study and prayer sessions. And when Donna welcomed the Holy Spirit into her life, supernatural encounters brought great strength and assurance. Donna prayed and fasted often for the family. And today, every family member serves God in some capacity.

Steppingstones of intercession presented themselves to Donna and brought her to Washington, D.C. for several years on the National Day of Prayer. Donna and a team from the Appalachian Conference of the IPCH were invited to participate in this yearly event. At these national prayer events, God's presence swept through the room, and touched the hearts of the intercessors.

A Unique Birth Announcement
(Mary – New Testament)

She didn't feel a thing. But in an instant, something took place in her body—something of cosmic proportions. The evidence of it would not be felt or seen immediately.

But within a few days she knew it had happened. With hands on her belly, Mary looked heavenward, seeing the vast blue sky afresh. Closing her eyes she embraced the warmth of the sun as it saturated her whole being. Sensing the wonder of Yahweh, she recalled the words of the angel, Gabriel, ***"For with God nothing shall be impossible"*** (Luke 1:37 KJV).

While she slept a holy thing had occurred just as Gabriel had said it would and inside the womb of this teenaged girl from the humble village of Nazareth, the presence of God suddenly resided. Literally, Mary's womb had become the Holy of Holies where God's own Son would gestate just like every human baby. God placed His own seed in her and there would grow Son of God/Son of Man for nine months.

Being told that she would be having a baby and knowing full well that she was a virgin, Mary responded, ***"Then said Mary to the angel, 'How can this be, seeing I know not a man?'"*** (Luke 1:34 KJV).

Gabriel answered her, saying, ***"The Holy Spirit will come upon you, and the power of the Highest will overshadow you, therefore, also, that Holy One who is to be born will be called the Son of God"*** (Luke 1:35).

After that, Gabriel told her that nothing is impossible with God: ***"Then Mary said, 'Behold the maidservant of the Lord! Let it be to me according to your word.' And the angel departed from her"*** (Luke 1:38).

The holy presence of Jesus growing inside Mary's womb was certainly a one-time occurrence and her faith-filled response to the angel's announcement is fascinating to me. Knowing the ramifications of being unmarried and pregnant in the First Century Jewish culture Mary accepted the charge amazingly well, in my opinion.

At her young age God saw in her the attributes of the chosen vessel He needed to bear and raise His only Son, along with her betrothed husband, Joseph.

When God calls us to an undertaking, we can be assured that He sees in us or will put in us the qualities, giftings, and potential to accomplish it. It is a holy thing to be called upon by the God of the universe to do a task. We can know that He will assist and need not turn Him down. Like Mary, let's say, ***"Let it be to me according to Your word,"*** and move forward in the direction He is leading.

Let's pray: *Holy Father, Your method of sending Jesus to us is amazing. In it we see evidence of Your omniscience and your great love and compassion. When You call on us to do hard or impossible things, please remind us, "For with God nothing shall be impossible." Thank You, Lord. In Jesus' name we pray—amen.*

Have you experienced a directive from God which you knew was an impossible task? If so, feel free to tell others about it using the hashtag, #HolyGroundAndMe

A Leaping Preborn Baby
(Elizabeth – New Testament)

When a verse in the Bible begins with the words, "And it happened," my interest is aroused. Something interesting, unusual, or alarming is coming next.

When the angel Gabriel visited the virgin Mary he revealed to her a second piece of important information—an announcement regarding another miracle in the works. ***"And behold, Elizabeth, your relative, has also conceived a son in her old age, and this is the sixth month for her who was called barren; for nothing will be impossible for God"*** (Luke 2:36-37). Immediately, Mary made preparations and hurried off to visit her cousin who lived in the hill country of Judah. Elizabeth didn't know of Mary's big news. From what we're told in Scripture Mary's visit was unannounced and unexpected.

Mary ***"entered the house of Zacharias and greeted Elizabeth. And it happened, when Elizabeth heard the greeting of Mary, that the babe leaped in her womb; and Elizabeth was filled with the Holy Spirit. Then she spoke out with a loud voice and said, 'Blessed are you among women, and blessed is the fruit of your womb! But why is this granted to me, that the mother of my Lord should come to me? For indeed, as soon as the voice of your greeting sounded in my ears, the babe leaped in my womb for joy'"*** (Luke 1:40-44).

What has happened here?

In the instant that Mary spoke to Elizabeth, John leaped inside Elizabeth's womb, and she knew the reason. A supernatural event had just taken place. Pre-born John and his mother, Elizabeth, encountered the very presence of the living God—their own Redeemer! It was a holy moment and was as if they had entered the Holy of Holies where God dwelt.

In that instant, Elizabeth was filled with the Holy Spirit. Both she and tiny little John knew, beyond any doubt, that the little One in Mary's belly was their longed-for Messiah. This elderly expectant mom along with her pre-born son had been granted spiritual vision—that is revelation knowledge as they encountered the God of Creation, the incarnate Son of God, Son of Man.

What we see here is a pregnant teen-aged virgin, Mary, and an elderly woman in her later months of pregnancy, Elizabeth, standing on holy ground. When Elizabeth heard Mary's voice her baby, who was John the Baptist, leaped within her, and she was filled with the Holy Spirit. By the Spirit, she instantly knew that God incarnate was growing in Mary's womb.

What an incredible holy moment which only God could orchestrate!

Elizabeth proclaimed, ***"Blessed is she who has believed that the Lord would fulfill his promises in her!"*** (Luke 1:45 NIV).

Let's pray: *Oh God, as we meditate on this experience of Elizabeth, pre-born John the Baptist, pre-born Jesus, and Mary, we see Your amazing workings in the lives of people You have chosen for special assignments. We see again that nothing is impossible with You. Help us to have revelation understanding of who You are, as well as Your truths and Your magnificence. Thank You, Lord, for Your living Word, Jesus, and in His name we pray, amen.*

Have you experienced a holy moment when God revealed something to you when you otherwise would not have known it? Please share your experience using the hashtag, #HolyGroundAndMe

Choose Life
(Lori)

"For You formed my inward parts; You covered me in my mother's womb, I will praise You, for I am fearfully and wonderfully made; Marvelous are Your works, and that my soul knows very well. ... Your eyes saw my substance, being yet unformed" (Psalm 139:13-14; 16a).

A little over 40 years ago in a small independent church, (Church of the Rock), my family was attending, I was introduced to teaching on the person of the Holy Spirit. Growing up, I was never taught such things though I went to church regularly. I was quite intrigued and eager to know more.

I wanted God's presence I my life and desired to be yielded to Him more and more. This was like a yearning, and it seemed that God was drawing me to a closer walk with Him. I was eager to yield to His pursuing.

It was during this time that I had a profound spiritual encounter that was life changing. I heard the audible voice of God! A couple of weeks prior to this occurrence, someone had given me a cassette tape with a hymn that resonated with me, and I heard it play over and over in my mind.

In the next Sunday service, our church had a missionary couple speak. The wife got up to sing a solo and said, "I have never sung this song before, but I feel led to sing it."

Well, it was that song I had been singing over and over. Then it happened. Suddenly, I heard an audible voice that seemed to thunder through my whole body—through my whole being. He said, "Abortion is taking human life!" The next thing I encountered was a sense of incredible grief to the point that I was sobbing. I was overcome with sadness because of the immense realization that abortion kills babies.

I already believed that abortion was wrong and that it took the lives of unborn babies, but this profound grief overwhelmed me. I couldn't control my sobbing.

On the way home I was explaining to my husband what had

happened to me while, at the same time, asking God, "What do You want me to do?" I knew I *had* to do something.

Within fifteen minutes of arriving home, I received a call from a lady from church, named Elizabeth. She asked if she could talk with me about information she had received from the Christian Action Council regarding Crisis Pregnancy Centers. Elizabeth was unaware of what had just happened to me at church and why I had cried. She was obviously being prompted by the Holy Spirit to contact me.

Soon after this we met with other pro-life people in our area who were interested in starting a local Crisis Pregnancy Center. Within a couple of years, the center opened to provide counseling and a wide array of services to pregnant girls and women experiencing unplanned pregnancies. After careful planning and much training, I had the privilege of serving there as a counselor for several years.

Knowing there are boys and girls, men and women alive on earth today because of my role at the center is extremely gratifying and something I thank God for continually. I had a hand in assisting women who were abortion minded change their minds and choose to give life to their unborn children. Plus, this freed them from the heartache and guilt that often plagues women who have had abortions.

I thank God for getting my attention on that memorable Sunday morning when I was overcome by His holy presence. His message changed the direction of my passions and my plans. I believe the plans and lives of many others were positively impacted also. Thank You, Lord!

Let's pray: *Oh Father, thank You for drawing us to You and leading us down the paths You desire and plan for each of us. Truly, Your ways are higher than our ways. Please bless the girls and women who choose life for their unborn babies and do provide everything they have need of. Oh God, please help those who have aborted their babies. Draw them to You—that they will receive Your great love and Your open arms of forgiveness. Help them to know that You are not mad at them and Your love is unconditional and unfailing. Help them to be made new through the shed blood of Christ Jesus. Thank You Heavenly Father. In Jesus' name we pray, amen.*

Are you a person who has had an abortion, paid for an abortion, or encouraged someone to have an abortion? Have you helped someone to recover from the trauma of abortion? Please share your thoughts using the hashtag, #HolyGroundAndMe

Seer, Dreamer, Interpreter, Beloved
(Daniel – Old Testament)

Though it happened many times, it was always breathtaking. It was overwhelming, mind-boggling, and sometimes strength sapping.

Swept away from his Jerusalem home, along with fellow Jews, teenaged Daniel purposed in his heart not to defile himself with the delicacies and vices of Babylonia. He had a made-up-mind that he would remain faithful to his God—Yahweh—the God of his fathers.

As the interpreter of King Nebuchadnezzar's dreams, he was elevated in position in the kingdom. Years rolled by and other kings came and went. Remaining faithful to God, Daniel experienced ups and downs but mostly found favor with the rulers.

Daniel and fellow Jews remained in captivity for seventy years, exactly as Ezekiel had prophesied. God began giving Daniel intensified prophetic and apocalyptic visions and interpretations. The fourth and last of his major visions had a profound effect on him. While by the Tigris River, he looked up and saw a man clothed in linen whose waist was girded with gold. The man's appearance was beyond human.

"His body also was like the beryl, and his face as the appearance of lightning, and his eyes as lamps of fire, and his arms and feet like in colour to polished brass, and the voice of his words like the voice of a multitude" (Daniel 10:6 KJV).

Daniel's companions didn't see the man but heard the sound of his voice. They fled in terror. As Daniel's strength and vigor drained from him, he fell into a deep sleep, yet continued to hear the man's words. He lay asleep face down on the ground.

"Suddenly a hand touched me, which made me tremble on my knees and on the palms of my hands. And he said to me. 'O Daniel, man greatly beloved, understand the words that I speak to you, and stand upright, for I have now been sent to you … Do not fear, Daniel, for from the first day that you set your heart to understand, and to humble yourself before your God, your words were heard; and I have come because of your words'" (Daniel 10:10-12).

As in times past, Daniel found himself in a holy moment on holy ground. Though not in the presence of God or Jesus, he was confronted by a holy messenger from the throne room of the Most High. He had received a message from God concerning the nation of Israel.

God's people were surrounded by evil. Sadly, many of His own turned away from their God giving in to the sin and worldliness around them. Through the messenger, God informed Daniel that those who forsook Him would pay a heavy price, but also encouraged Daniel that a remnant of the faithful would always exist.

"And such as do wickedly against the covenant shall he corrupt by flatteries: but the people that do know their God shall be strong, and do exploits" (Daniel 11:32 KJV).

But they won't have it easy. The angel went on to say that many people *"shall fall by the sword and by flame, by captivity and by spoil, many days"* (Daniel 1:33b KJV).

The very last verse in The Book of Daniel gives him a personal word of encouragement: *"But you, go your way till the end; for you shall rest, and arise to your inheritance at the end of the days"* (Daniel 12:13).

Through many hardships and the sadness of witnessing the downfall of Jerusalem and the captivity of his people, Daniel remained faithful to his youthful promises to God. It is believed that Daniel lived into his eighties. His long-term devotion to God was Daniel's legacy. He had many qualities we would do well to emulate. We can be assured that God honors and rewards obedience and faithfulness. Over and over Daniel proved himself to be that upstanding man of God.

Let's pray: *Oh God, thank You for providing us with the experiences of Daniel and for allowing us to see your hand working in the affairs of Mankind. We're so encouraged to see that you prophesied events and then we look at history and know that Your words and predictions were right on target. How encouraging and faith building that is for us. Thank You for your forever faithfulness. In Jesus' name we pray, amen.*

Have you experienced a remarkable visitation of an angel, dispatched from God's throne room to deliver a message just for you? Perhaps it was an instruction, a word of comfort or encouragement. If so, please share your experience using the hashtag, #HolyGroundAndMe.

[Side Note: Only twelve chapters in length, please read the entire Book of Daniel. Be amazed at his interpretations of dreams. Be astonished at the visions God gave him. Be fascinated by the prophesies that came to pass years later. Be encouraged by the strength of character of youthful Daniel becoming old man Daniel, faithful to the end. He knew his God and that Yahweh was his source.]

Silent Seer
(Gary S.)

"Call to Me and I will answer you and show you great and mighty things, [things which have been confined and hidden], which you do not know and understand and cannot distinguish" (Jeremiah 33:3 AMP).

Although I did not know that I was a Seer until I was 35, looking back now I realize that my first experience was during Vacation Bible School the summer between 3rd and 4th grades. As a third grader I had achieved a reading level that permitted me to read simple passages from the Bible. After I read my selection aloud to the small class, I was then asked what I thought it meant. My mind was flooded with pictures. I simply told the teacher and class what I was seeing. I received stares and no one said anything. Being in a traditional Lutheran church there was no one who could say what I was seeing was prophetic nor encourage me to continue. So, although I continued to read the Bible and see pictures and visions, I did not tell anyone and kept the meanings to myself. I was silent.

By the time I reached the 6th grade, I became aware of famous architects that seemed to see visions of pictures of the future. My conclusion was that perhaps I was going to grow up to be an architect. Later in high school I discovered visionary engineers and urban planners. At least I was beginning to have an avenue to express to others some of the pictures of the future I was seeing in my mind, without telling them their meanings. It was like I was interpreting what I was seeing without offending others.

In my late teens and twenties, I found that as I met people, I could use the pictures I was seeing about people's future to give them compliments that they seemed to like. As I began my university teaching career at age twenty-five, I would often talk to some of my students, and they would ask me about what they should do about plans they had. I would see visions of where they should go, who they should talk to, who they should collaborate with, etc. I would simply offer them advice by interpreting what I was seeing, but in a very low-key manner.

Often students would seek me out after summer break and come tell me in the fall that they did what I suggested they do, and it worked! I would often meet former students several years later and they would say they remembered the day I gave them advice and they had become very successful following my advice. Ironically, I also saw pictures and visions of myself several decades in advance that I stored away to see what actually materialized.

My story now jumps to age thirty-five. During the previous ten years I had gotten married, started a family, lost my first wife to a sudden illness, was a widower with two young children, and remarried a good friend of mine. My second wife was also raised in the Lutheran church but was recently born again in the Baptist church. We were both awakening to the Spirit and although we were attending both a Lutheran church and a Baptist church, we started to joke about, "Are we ready to try that crazy charismatic Methodist church in town." One Sunday morning we woke up and said, "Let's try crazy today," and we did.

My wife was immediately excited about the service of contemporary music and even dancing in the aisles. As the music and service started, I was flooded with overwhelming visions. After the service was over, I was exhausted and immediately went home and went to bed and did not wake up until Monday morning. For the next few weeks, we tried again with both of us having the same results as the first week. My wife finally concluded that we needed to go talk to the pastor about what was happening to me each Sunday.

Upon attending our appointment with the pastor and describing what was happening to me during and after the service, he jumped up and said, "Can you come with me to a deliverance service going on right now?" Not knowing what that meant, we said, "Yes." What we discovered was that we were being invited to a home church deliverance service. As I participated in the service, I felt a heavy fog of oppression being lifted off me. We talked after the service and the pastor asked me to attend the men's prayer service the next Sunday to pray for the pastor during the hour before the services.

I did attend the men's prayer service. At the end of the prayers the pastor asked if anyone had anything else to say. I meekly raised my hand and said that I had seen a vision. He told me to feel free to share it. The gist of the vision was, "I saw injured birds in our community using crutches to walk into our church and injured wings with bandages fly weakly into our church. Inside there was a bonfire of bright blue starlight. The birds would enter the blue light and come out healed and carrying a small stone of the blue light. Then they would fly out through a special opening in the roof and fly over the community and surrounding territory and drop there stone, which ignited small campfires for other birds to come for healing." The pastor passionately told me to write down that vision and bring it next week when we were going to have a guest pastor speak.

The next Sunday the guest pastor attended the men's prayer meeting for our pastor. My pastor introduced me to the guest pastor and indicated the two of us needed to discuss the vision I had the previous week. We chatted briefly and then I told him my vision. When I finished, he simply looked at me and said, "You are a Seer." The guest pastor was a prophet named Chuck Pierce. He then told me what my vision meant and explained what it meant to be a Seer. He explained that I have had the gift of a Seer most of my life and that the gift would become stronger and stronger now that I understood its purpose and application. He said a Seer was a Prophet that could see what the Lord was doing in the lives of individuals and groups of people.

The events of those ten days opened my mind to the gifts of the Spirit and began to give me confidence that what I was seeing was worth saying. I began to befriend others in this new church of ours who were also exercising their spiritual gifts so that I could learn by watching and learn by doing.

A few months later I was attending a conference where my pastor was the main speaker. During his opening remarks at 9 AM he stopped and pointed to me in the audience and said that if anyone wanted to know what plans the Lord had for them, they should come speak to me. A small group immediately gathered around me, so I was instructed to relocate to a quiet space backstage. I had a couple of people act as intercessors and I began to have individuals come and sit with the three of us. As I would have a vision for them, I would say what I was seeing, and it was recorded for them to take with them. Three hours passed and it was lunch time, but there were as many people waiting as when we started at 9 AM. So, someone brought me some lunch while I continued to minister. The afternoon passed and it was time for the evening meal, but again the line was no shorter. The same person brought me some dinner as I continued to minister. Finally, the daily conference ended at 10 PM, when I finished with the final individuals.

In the forty years that have followed I have occasionally ministered in small group congregational gatherings, but the vast majority of my Seer encounters have been in private personal and business settings. For some people I have seen them in a robe with ornaments, badges, and jewelry on them that turned out to have specific and valuable meanings to them. For others I have described a very specific looking house that they were desiring to purchase but were afraid to make a decision. For some I described a business partner that would lead both of them into a successful lifetime business collaboration. For one woman, the Lord saw her as a mother of the lost children of a small community and He wanted to give her favor to establish a foster home for them.

Currently He is showing me people who should develop Kingdom friendships which will lead to covenant relationships with Kingdom assignments to establish the Kingdom of Heaven on the Earth. He is introducing those who have the plans to those who have the resources. By *Saying* what I am *Seeing*, the visions are the magnets to attract the provisions.

We all appreciate hearing stories of Holy events happening on Holy ground that dramatically change the directions of lives. Looking back over my lifetime, I have mostly stayed on the Favor Path on Holy ground and have encountered a series of Holy events which have accumulated to guide my direction. The Lord used my Silent Seer youth years as training for what was released in my mid-thirties when, within a few weeks, He opened my eyes to my role as a prophetic Seer. Certainly, the declaring word of prophecy and encouragement from Prophet Chuck Pierce increased my confidence for my gift but also helped prepare me for my Kingdom assignment, now thirty years later. As a bonus, having my wife grow spiritually with me from Chuck Pierce and onward has allowed her to be very supportive and encouraging for me in my assignments.

Let's pray: *Holy Father, we thank You that You know the end before the beginning; You know our coming in and our going out; Your ways are higher than our ways. We thank You that You are well able to do more than we can ever ask, think, or imagine and You are trustworthy. Help us to hear You clearly and follow You with clear vision and Your truth in discerning. In Jesus' name we pray, amen.*

Are you a Seer? Has God shown you things in your spirit in a supernatural way? How did you know this was from God and not just your own imagination? Feel free to tell us about your experiences using the hashtag, #HolyGroundAndMe

Be Strong and Courageous
(Joshua – Old Testament)

The commission was clear, and the directive was succinct. One of history's most consequential if-then statements was pronounced by the very Creator of the Universe. And three times He said to Joshua, *"Be strong and courageous."*

God commissioned Joshua, starting out by saying, *"Moses My servant is dead; Now therefore, arise, go over this Jordan, thou and all this people, unto the land which I do give to them, even to the children of Israel"* (Joshua 1:2 KJV).

God then described the expanse of that land—the land He had told Ezekiel was, *"the glory of all lands"* (Ezekiel 20:6b).

In the next few verses, we see God encourage Joshua by affirming they would have victory over their enemies along the way and boosted his confidence telling him, *"as I was with Moses, so I will be with you. I will not leave you nor forsake you"* (Joshua 1:5b).

God repeated it in the next two verses: *"Be strong and of good courage …"* In verse seven, God said, *"Only be thou strong and very courageous …"* (Joshua 1:6a; 7a KJV).

This omniscient God knew the frailties of men. He knew that strength and courage would be necessary to accomplish the tasks ahead. Even with the presence of God the Israelite armies would need inward resolve. But the charge was conditional. If the children of Israel would follow God's instructions, then they would realize victory and dwell in the land which would be their own.

God said, *"Only be strong and very courageous, that you may observe to do according to all the law which Moses My servant commanded you; do not turn from it to the right hand or to the left, that you may prosper wherever you go. This Book of the Law shall not depart from your mouth, but you shall meditate in it day and night, that you may observe to do according to all that is written in it. For then you will make your way prosperous, and then you will have good success. Have I not commanded you? Be strong and of good courage; do not be afraid, nor be dismayed, for the LORD your God is with you wherever you go"* (Joshua 1:7-9).

Joshua informed the leaders and preparations began. He passed on God's instructions and repeated God's words, *"Only be strong and of good courage"* (v. 18b).

The time came to cross over Jordan and take the first city in the land which God had promised. That city was Jericho, a heavily fortified walled city and God had a plan.

[Side note: Just as God had done about forty years earlier with Moses at the Red Sea, He opened the waters for the Israelites now at the Jordan River and they crossed over on dry land. Read about this miraculous event in Joshua 3:5-17.]

The plan was set and the time for action drew near. The Ark of the Covenant was in place; the seven priests bearing seven trumpets of rams' horns were made ready; the people were ready to shout when the signal was given; and the army was ready to move.

"And it came to pass, when Joshua was by Jericho, that he lifted up his eyes and looked, and behold, a Man stood opposite him with His sword drawn in His hand. And Joshua went to Him and said to Him, 'Are You for us or for our adversaries?'

"So He said, 'No, but as Commander of the army of the LORD I have come.' And Joshua fell on his face to the earth and worshiped, and said to Him, 'What does my Lord say to His servant?'

"Then the Commander of the LORD's army said to Joshua, 'Take your sandel off your foot, for the place where you stand is holy.' And Joshua did so" (Joshua 5:13-15).

The Commander of commanders had arrived. Any anxiety Joshua might have been experiencing prior to this holy moment was bound to have dissipated. The Holy One of Israel was present and in charge.

"So the people shouted when the priests blew the trumpets. And then it happened when the people heard the sound of the trumpet, and the people shouted with a great shout, that the wall fell down flat. Then the people went up into the city, every man straight before him, and they took the city" (Joshua 6:20).

That day marked the beginning of the children of Israel dwelling in their own land, fulfilling centuries of prophesies. Joshua knew he had heard from God and by faith was moving forward in God's plan. Then when the Commander of Heaven's armies showed up, he could do nothing but fall on his face and worship.

Through the obedience of Joshua and the people Jehovah God was pleased and victory was theirs. God had made it clear that *if* they would do this His way, *then* they would be victorious. When we read the entire account, we might think that some of God's instructions did not seem logical to man's thinking. But God knew exactly how the victory needed to come about and wanted Joshua and the people to focus on Him and His Word as they trusted His ways.

Let's pray: *Oh God, like Joshua and the children of Israel, may we observe to do according to Your will. With the help of the Holy Spirit, may we never let Your commandments, and Your Word depart from our mouths. Thank You for giving us victories as we honor You with our lives. In Jesus' name, amen.*

Have you experienced a time when God told you that if you will do something according to His ways, then the outcome would be good? If so, please share it with us on social media using the hashtag, #HolyGroundAndMe

Stand Still and See
(Jehoshaphat – Old Testament)

It was not a good situation, and the prospects of survival were slim to none. Jehoshaphat listened intently as his informant announced that a coalition of enemy armies was headed toward Jerusalem.

"And Jehoshaphat feared, and set himself to seek the LORD, and proclaimed a fast throughout all Judah" (2 Chronicles 20:3 KJV).

So, the people gathered together to appeal to Heaven. From all the cities of Judah they came. Jehoshaphat stood before the assembly in the house of the LORD and said: *"O LORD God of our fathers, are You not God in heaven, and do You not rule over all the kingdoms of the nations, and in Your hand is there not power and might, so that no one is able to withstand you? Are You not our God, who drove out the inhabitants of the land before Your people Israel, and gave it to the descendants of Abraham Your friend forever?"* (2 Chronicles 20:6-7).

Jehoshaphat's plea is recorded in its entirety in 2 Chronicles 20:6-12. It ends with *"nor do we know what to do, but our eyes are upon You."*

The God of Israel heard the heart cries of the king and the people.

Then it happened. A holy moment occurred when the Holy Spirit came upon Jahaziel, a Levite, who stood among the people. He had received an answer from God and said, *"'Listen, all you of Judah and you inhabitants of Jerusalem, and you, King Jehoshaphat! Thus says the LORD to you: 'Do not be afraid nor dismayed because of this great multitude, for the battle is not yours, but God's. Tomorrow go down against them ...'"* (2 Chronicles 20:15).

Then the Lord gave them the location and the battle strategy. God concluded His instruction saying, *"'You will not need to fight this battle. Position yourselves, stand still and see the salvation of the LORD, who is with you, O Judah and Jerusalem! Do not fear or be dismayed; tomorrow go out against them, for the LORD is with you.' And Jehoshaphat bowed his head with his face to the ground, and all Judah and the inhabitants of Jerusalem bowed before the LORD, worshipping the LORD"* (2 Chronicles 20:17-18).

Then all the people stood and lifted their voices with loud praises to God, trusting Him to fight the battle and rescue them from their strong enemies.

The next morning King Jehoshaphat appointed certain people to sing to the Lord and others to lift praises to God and the beauty of His holiness. *"Now when they began to sing and praise, the LORD set ambushes against the people of Ammon, Moab, and Mount Seir, who had come against Judah; and they were defeated"* (2 Chronicles 20:22).

Not only that, those armies began to turn on each other, until all were annihilated. No one got away. That wilderness area was covered in dead bodies, and it took three days for the people of Judah to gather all the spoils, which was abundant according to verse twenty-five.

On the fourth day the victorious people gathered at the house of the Lord in Jerusalem to celebrate with stringed instruments, harps, and trumpets. We can just imagine the joyous event. Just a week earlier these people of God feared for their lives and their possessions. A massive army was heading their way with bloodshed on their minds. Their plan was to utterly destroy the inhabitants of Judah.

But Judah had a king who knew his God—a king who fed his faith rather than his fear—a king who immediately turned to the God of his fathers. King Jehoshaphat gathered the people and appealed to Heaven, to the throne room of God Almighty. He knew the history of Yahweh and his forefathers.

That holy moment when King Jehoshaphat cried out to God in faith altered the circumstances they were in and moved them from hopeless to hopeful. The people stood and bowed down on holy ground lifting their life and death petitions up to God. Then, what a holy moment it was when Jahaziel heard from God, proclaiming the victory awaiting them.

Let's pray: *Oh, Mighty God, I want to be like Jehoshaphat and immediately turn to You when trouble is on my horizon. Help me to continually feed my faith rather than my fear every day, so that when big threats come, I'm established in You and ready to put situations into Your hands. Thank You for Your great love for me and my loved ones and that You are my trustworthy King. In Jesus' name, amen.*

Have you experienced a circumstance where if God had not stepped in it would have been all over? Maybe it was literally life and death, perhaps a marriage on the verge of annihilation, or a situation of impending financial disaster. Did you appeal to Heaven immediately? Please share your experience using the hashtag, #HolyGroundAndMe

God Will Make a Way
(Laura)

In the Spring of 2005, I married my high school sweetheart, knowing in my heart, it was the wrong decision for my spiritual future. He was an atheist, and I had fallen far away from God. But of course, I knew I had all the time in the world to make things right. I still prayed and asked Him for help when I needed it, but that was the extent of my relationship with Jesus. I was an alcoholic, drinking most days until I didn't remember going to bed, fighting with my new husband, spending nights alone in our new home while he stayed out drinking with his friends; wondering if he would come home or stay with some woman he met in one of the bars he frequented.

In the summer of 2006, I found myself pregnant with our first child. It was July 8th, and I didn't feel quite right. I took a pregnancy test and though we had been trying for a baby, I was shocked to see the two pink lines. We had only been trying for a couple of months. I felt like I was unworthy to have a child seeing how I wasn't living a life that God would be proud of and certainly didn't deserve to be blessed with a baby. On that very afternoon, at a stoplight in Williamsburg, VA, I rededicated my life to Jesus. His Spirit washed over me as I was turning into the Chili's parking lot to tell my husband that I was pregnant. I felt a peace come over me that assured me I was going to be a mother and have a child to be responsible for. In my mind, it would change things. I would do better. I would go to church. He would want to come with me, and we would raise our child knowing Christ like I did when I was young. Together we would give thanks for God's faithfulness. Boy was I wrong!

My husband would NOT let me go to church. He didn't want me to be "brainwashed" by those people and absolutely did not want his child to be subject to the nonsense that was Christianity. His drinking got worse, and I was scared. He had always been verbally and physically abusive and that got worse as well. He would go days without coming home, only to stumble into the house at 3a.m. on a Monday morning demanding clean clothes and breakfast so he could go to work. Or he would beat me or rape me. I was scared for my life and the life of my unborn daughter. I remember one instance locking myself in our bathroom and crying on the toilet while he tried to bust down the door. I apologized to my unborn daughter for bringing her into this world and that I wished I had the courage to leave him. But I didn't know what I would do or where I would go.

Our daughter was born in March of 2007. She was perfect in every single way. She didn't cry, she was beautiful and was just what my soul needed. I would talk to her quietly every night and thank her for "saving" me from myself and addiction because she really did. If I hadn't gotten pregnant with her, I would have still been drinking heavily every night with my husband. I just knew things would be different with him now that he had a daughter to take care of too! But I was so wrong. His drinking got out of control. He would come home so drunk he would pass out in his car, or in the yard. He would go days without any contact, and I was at home alone to take care of a newborn. I would go home to my parents' house four hours away just to get away from him. I would then come home to a trashed house and evidence he'd had different women in my bed. I was so devastated.

I left him for the first time when our daughter was five months old and moved in with my parents for a month. He agreed to marriage counseling. After just two sessions he said he wouldn't go back. I resumed the day-to-day routine of working part time and holding my breath when he got home. I never knew if he was going to be drunk and ready to beat up on me or be in a good mood and play with the baby pretending things were okay.

I knew I didn't want to have more children with my husband. Things weren't going well yet I didn't have the courage to leave him. I was just trying to survive and raise my daughter the best I could with what I had. He still wouldn't let us go to church, so I would only attend when I traveled to Radford to see my parents. I was on birth control, and we rarely had intercourse since he was drunk most of the time. Besides that, I didn't know who he was with most weekends. Since I was still breastfeeding our daughter, I felt that the chances of me getting pregnant were close to zero.

Then it happened. The Monday after Easter Sunday in 2008, while driving from work to get our daughter from the babysitter, I heard the Lord speak to me. He said, "Trust Me." I had just heard the audible voice of God! Time stood still in that holy moment. Just two words—I had no idea what He meant but I knew it was God.

I picked up my daughter and went home but just felt like something was *off*. I took a pregnancy test the next day because I realized I had missed a period. It was faint but positive. I was gutted. How was I going to tell him? He would kill me, for sure. I set up a video camera and called my sister. I told her about the pregnancy and told her that if she hadn't heard from me within the hour to call the police, that something bad had happened. To this day, I still have that video of me telling him I was pregnant. It didn't go over very well, but he didn't hit me. He simply pulled out a bottle of liquor, chugged half of it and disappeared for a few days.

A few weeks later I was in the doctor's office. The normal tests were run, and the nurse asked twice if I was sure I had a positive pregnancy test. I told her I had taken two, they were faint, but that I was sure. She then ordered a blood test and had me wait for the doctor. I had honestly forgotten about God speaking to me that Monday telling me to trust Him, but then it flooded through my mind as I waited alone in that room. I didn't know what was going on, but I knew my God had a plan.

The doctor came in and told me that my tests came back and that I was miscarrying the baby. His exact words were, "I hope you haven't told anyone you're pregnant, you're going to lose this pregnancy soon." I was so upset. I had told my sister and parents. I of course didn't WANT another child but also the loss of a baby was just devastating. I left the doctor's office in tears, grieving a child that I hadn't met yet. But in the back of my mind, I kept God's words close. "Trust ME."

Eight weeks later, I went into my obstetrician's office for a follow-up and an ultrasound. A strong heartbeat and a wiggly little bean showed up. The doctor looked at me and said, "Well, this one's a fighter; I didn't think he'd make it." Then the doctor looked at me and made the most impactful statement to me that I had heard in my life. As he looked at my bruised face he said, "If you don't leave your situation right now, you WILL lose this baby and possibly your own life."

It was in that moment I knew I had to go. I HAD to trust God and pick up what I could and leave. God had given me a child so I would have the courage to leave for good and create a new life for the children He was blessing me with. God knew I wouldn't leave on my own accord, so He made a way for me to find the strength. He knew every mother must protect her children from anything threatening them and fight for their safety, their eternity, their very lives. I don't know how He made it possible for that little fella to be created that spring of 2008, but he turns sixteen this year and is the most incredible young man. He loves Jesus and is such a light for Christ. God's plans are always so much greater than we can imagine. I am so thankful for His faithfulness in my life and the lives of my children. We left a terrible situation and have been blessed now for 16 years!

*"**Thus says the Lord, who makes a way in the sea and a path through the mighty waters. … 'Do not remember the former things, nor consider the things of old. Behold, I will do a new thing, Now it shall spring forth; shall you not know it? I will even make a road in the wilderness And rivers in the desert.'"** (Isaiah 43:16, 18-19).*

Let's pray: *Wonderful Heavenly Father, thank You for keeping Your hand on me and my precious children and for providing a way for us through the wilderness. I know that if You will do this for my family You will do it for others as well all because of Your great love. Please minister to those who are hurting and being hurt. I know that Your arm is not too short and that You can make a way for life and hope for every single one in need. Thank You, Holy God. I praise You and glorify Your holy name. In Your name, King Jesus, I pray, amen.*

Are you in an abusive situation and in need of prayer? Do you want God to give you direction about what to do? Our Creator knows, He sees, and He cares. Feel free to share your thoughts using the hashtag, #HolyGroundAndMe

Broken and Restored
(Sinful Woman with Flask of Perfume
- New Testament)

"Your faith has saved you. Go in peace," were the priceless words Jesus spoke to her. She had entered the house covered in shame and left the house covered in grace. Never before had such kind words been spoken to her.

Known to be a sinful woman, disgraced because of her lifestyle, she entered the home of Simon, a Pharisee, where Jesus was a dinner guest.

"And behold, a woman in the city who was a sinner, when she knew that Jesus sat at the table in the Pharisee's house, brought an alabaster flask of fragrant oil, and stood at His feet behind Him weeping; and she began to wash His feet with her tears, and wiped them with the hair of her head; and she kissed His feet and anointed them with the fragrant oil" (Luke 7:37-38).

Broken and repentant, this woman whose name we don't even know recognized who Jesus was. All her hope was in Him. Tears of sorrow for her past deeds flowed as she knelt at His feet. With reckless abandon she worshiped Him on holy ground in the home of a Pharisee who himself didn't see with spiritual eyes as she did.

Heavy fragrance filled the home when she broke open the flask. Christ's love filled her emptiness as her broken spirit and contrite heart lay bare before Him, as well as everyone else in the room. In an instant her spirit received the freedom of forgiveness available only through Jesus.

A broken flask of oil
A broken heart of sin
A Savior full of love
A woman born again.

Disturbed by this, the Pharisee host questioned Jesus, saying that if He was a true prophet He'd have known what manner of woman she was. His critical spirit could not see beneath the surface, but Jesus could see Simon's prideful heart just as He could see the woman's contrite heart. Jesus put him in his place and by His response we learn that Simon had not performed common courtesies one would offer a guest.

"And Jesus answered and said to him, 'Simon, I have something to say to you.' So he said, 'Teacher, say it'" (Luke 7:40).

Jesus told a parable of one who owed a great debt and one who owed a small debt. Their creditor freely forgave each of their entire debt.

Jesus went on to say, *"Tell Me therefore, which of them will love him more?"* (Luke 7:43b).

Simon correctly answered that the one with the greater debt would be the most grateful.

Then Jesus said, *"'Do you see this woman? I entered your house; you gave Me no water for my feet, but she washed My feet with her tears and wiped them with the hair of her head. You gave Me no kiss, but this woman has not ceased to kiss My feet since the time I came in. You did not anoint My head with oil, but this woman has anointed My feet with fragrant oil. Therefore I say to you, her sins, which are many, are forgiven, for she loved much. But to whom little is forgiven, the same loves little'"* (Luke 7:44b-47).

"Then He said to the woman, 'Your faith has saved you. Go in peace'" (Luke 7:50).

This woman's spirit connected with the Spirit of Jesus, the Son of the living God and she knew who He was and why He came. She apparently had previous familiarity with Jesus and was drawn to Him by the Holy Spirit. She knew she needed a Savior and discerned Him as the One who could meet her needs.

Like her encounter at Jesus' feet in sincere repentance is what we each need. He desires to meet us where we are and say to us, *"Your faith has saved you. Go in peace."* The place where we repent and relinquish ourselves to the forgiving Savior is truly holy ground and the holy moment of being born-again. We are then translated from death to life—from darkness to light. The Light of the World has become our Redeemer.

Have you come to that place of recognizing who Jesus is—that He is the Son of the living God? Like the woman in this account, have you recognized that you're a sinner in need of a Savior? Right now is the perfect time to receive Jesus into your heart and be born-again if you haven't already done so. We're not promised tomorrow. Don't put it off. Today is the day of salvation.

Let's pray: *Holy Father, wonderful Savior, thank You for offering total forgiveness to anyone who will believe and receive Your free gift of salvation. I'm so sorry for my sins as I kneel at Your feet in humble gratitude. All I have to give You is my whole self and I offer that up to You now. Thank You for drawing me to You and for Your saving grace. In Jesus' name I pray, amen.*

Have you received Jesus into your heart today? If so, PRAISE God! We rejoice with you! Whether it was just now or sometime in the past, please share your experience on social media using the hashtag, #HolyGroundAndMe

Delivered
(Liz Dickson)

I sat there as tears streamed down my face, wondering if the people around me saw the blubbering mess I was. This wasn't the norm for me. Actually, it wasn't normal at all for me because generally, I never cried. I had decided there wasn't any reason to cry because no one cared.

The preacher stopped preaching and asked if anyone would like to come up for prayer. My friend who invited me to church turned to me and asked me if I'd like to go to the altar. The alter—that wasn't a familiar term to me, but I knew I was supposed to go.

As I got up from my seat and headed to the front, even though there was a church full of people I felt like I was the only one in the room. I walked up front with one intention in mind—just to be there. I didn't know what would happen when I got there. I just felt so drawn—a feeling I had never experienced before. Looking back on that day it's as if Jesus was leading me down that isle and we were the only two in that little country church that evening.

I knelt down just as others were doing across the front of the church. I remember hearing the preacher praying for each one. That was also foreign to me. In my eighteen years of life, I'd never heard someone pray out loud for anyone. He touched their heads and prayed a very forceful prayer for each.

It was my turn. He asked me if I'd like him to pray for me. Of course, I said, "Yes."

I didn't know what was happening to me up to this point so I must have needed prayer. He then asked would I like to be saved. Without even fully understanding what he meant, I said, "Yes." I knew I needed to be saved from the horrible life I was living. He and his wife laid their hands on me and prayed.

Then it happened. I don't remember anything that was said but I do remember the feeling that engulfed me. When I stood up from that place—that holy place—I felt like a million pounds came off me. It was like all Hell lifted off of me. I didn't know Scriptures at that time, but I now know that the best way to describe what I felt was that I was a new creation in Christ Jesus. The old man had passed away and behold ALL was new!

It happened just as Paul describes in 2 Corinthians 5:17: ***"Therefore, if anyone is in Christ, he is a new creation; old things have passed away; behold, all things have become new."***

I not only felt different. I talked different, and I thought different. I had no desire for the things I was so deeply bound up in before that night. It was a supernatural deliverance—one of which I would never even have imagined could happen to me—a sinner like me!

Today, it's been thirty-four years since I confessed Christ Jesus as my Savior. All praise and honor goes to Him. I have come to know Him as Friend, Healer, Provider, Counselor, and loving Heavenly Father. I'm so thankful He saw fit to stop everything around me that night and draw me to him.

My life was changed forever. The trajectory of my life was altered that night. Instead of a path heading for destruction, God lead me down a path of abundant life filled with family, friends, ministry, and more.

I'm forever grateful for God's amazing grace, His unconditional love, and His delivering power. I don't understand how a person enslaved to sin like I was can be transformed in a moment, but I now know that God's wonder working power is real. He saw me in my misery and welcomed me into His own family in that instant. I simply had to say, "Yes."

Do you need to say, "Yes" to God—to say "Yes" to Jesus? —to say "Yes" I believe in You, Jesus, and I want You to save me from the destruction of my sins? If so, just do it and invite Jesus to live in your heart and welcome His Spirit to fill you with the fullness of Him.

Let's pray: *Father God, thank You for loving me so much that You reached down and picked me up out of a life of sin and destruction. Please fill me and help me, Holy Spirit, to walk in the newness of abundant life that You want me to have. In Jesus' mighty name I pray, amen.*

Have you experienced the delivering power of Christ Jesus? Your encounter may not have been as intense as Liz's, but I expect it was life altering. Or would you like for us to pray for you at this time? Please share your thoughts using the hashtag, #HolyGroundAndMe

Two Who Knew
(Simeon and Anna – New Testament)

He had a deep desire to see the promised Messiah before he died. As an old man, Simeon had not forgotten the promise God had made him. He continued to wait and watch for the Consolation of Israel—the Deliverer who would bring comfort to God's chosen people. (Luke 2:25-26).

And then it happened.

"So he (Simeon) came by the Spirit into the temple. And when the parents brought in the Child Jesus, to do for Him according to the custom of the law, he took Him up in his arms and blessed God and said: 'Lord, now You are letting Your servant depart in peace, According to Your word; for my eyes have seen Your salvation which You have prepared before the face of all peoples, A light to bring revelation to the Gentiles, and the glory of Your people Israel,'" (Luke 2:27-32).

Joseph and Mary were a bit stunned. They had not been expecting such a confirmation that this forty-day old baby boy they were bringing to be dedicated was indeed the Christ. His being recognized by a total stranger gave them much to ponder as they continued further into the temple.

Then it happened again.

Eighty-four-year-old Anna had been a widow for many years. A devout prophetess, she *"did not depart from the temple, but served God with fastings and prayers night and day. And coming in that instant she gave thanks to the Lord and spoke of Him to all those who looked for redemption in Jerusalem"* (Luke 2:37b-38).

Anna was given the blessing of a lifetime. In that holy moment, near the end of her days, she beheld her Messiah and proclaimed Him to all who were near.

Through His Spirit, God revealed and then with their physical eyes Simeon and Anna each received the revelation of God's Salvation. Right in front of them was a little baby Who was the Light of the world to both Jew and Gentile—the Redemption God had promised centuries earlier. For each of them it was a holy moment. They each found themselves standing on holy ground, in the presence, face to face with God incarnate. From that moment on they would never be the same for God had not forgotten the promises He had given each of them in their younger years—that they would not die before seeing the Promised One.

The One Isaiah referred to as the Holy One of Israel had come and visited them. All their desires were satisfied. Be assured that He came to satisfy our desires too.

Let's pray: *Oh Father, thank You for showing us these wonderful experiences of Simeon and Anna. Imagining their delight brings satisfaction to our own hearts. Help us to also have revelation of who Jesus is to the point that we proclaim Him to those around us. In Jesus' name, amen.*

If you have come to realize, in a holy moment, when you knew in your knower that Jesus is the Christ please share your experience using the hashtag, #HolyGroundAndMe

God is Faithful in My Unfaithfulness (William)

Growing up, I lived in a Christian household. My father and grandmother especially pointed me and my siblings to God daily, as they are devout followers of Jesus. They showed the characteristics of Christ and were a testimony of His love. So, when I was in third grade, I asked Jesus to enter into my heart and I told my grandmother I wanted to be baptized.

From then on, I had always believed in Jesus. Yes, doubts were a factor in my faith at times especially when I was young, but never did I not believe. However, I didn't know fully how to live a life committed to Christ.

During my high school years was when I really started to stray away from the Lord. I knew I was doing things that didn't please God. But with conviction from the Holy Spirit as well as God using circumstances in my life, He always called me and led me back to Him. He put people in my life and took me places that helped me to learn and grow in my faith. Though my flesh is strong, and in my younger years I was quick to give into its desires, the Lord was constantly refining me, and He still is. He has proven Himself faithful in my unfaithfulness.

The summer after my freshman year of college I went to a discipleship program in Tennessee through Young Life, and it played a huge role in the growing of my faith. It was like that place was holy ground and God was doing a holy work in me. I learned what it means to follow Jesus as well as the importance of community.

God was answering many questions that had been swirling around in my brain. I had been wondering about the purpose of life and trying to intellectualize the Gospel. Why did I think I could figure God out?

I was learning just what Proverbs 3:5-6 says: ***"Trust in the Lord with all your heart, And lean not on your own understanding; In all your ways acknowledge Him, And He shall direct your paths."***

I concluded that I do want God to direct my path. He knows the way that's best for me. In that discipleship program I had deep conversations in a small group with other college guys. I gained a better understanding that we are each created by God for a purpose. We have a choice and God is not into mind-control of His people. We have free choice about following Him or not.

I gained a better understanding of what sin is. It is when we do not serve that purpose and we do our own will, thus separating us from God. Thank God for mercy and grace!

The best part is that I gained a better understanding of God's sacrificial Lamb, His Son, Jesus Christ, and what He did on the cross to take the penalty I deserve for all my sins—past, present, and future. Our response is what we believe about Him. Do we believe in Jesus or not?

Since then, I have been more involved with Young Life and have become a leader for teen boys. Also, I'm involved with my church community, as well as investing in my personal relationship with God.

I want to be the man of God that He created me to be. I know I must be pro-active in that pursuit. Therefore, I continue in prayer, reading and studying Scripture, and worshiping my Creator. Through those things, I know I am abiding in Jesus. Jesus said, ***"I am the vine, you are the branches. He who abides in Me, and I in Him, bears much fruit; for without Me you can do nothing"*** (John 15:5).

Let's pray: *Oh Father, thank You that You don't give up on us. You never forgot my third-grade commitment to You and You never let me forget it either. Thank You for putting people in my life to encourage, teach, and disciple me, helping me grow in faith. Especially thank You for Your Holy Spirit who forever draws me and comforts me. Help me to hear Your voice clearly and boldly walk in Your ways. In Jesus' name, amen.*

Are you one who made a profession of faith in Christ or made a commitment to God at a young age and then strayed somewhat or even a lot? Have you renewed your profession of faith in Jesus and your commitment to Him? Feel free to tell us about your experience, using the hashtag, #HolyGroundAndMe

They Forsook All and Followed Him
(Peter – New Testament)

There will be days like this. Whether you're a car salesman, a restauranteur, or a fisherman—not a single sale, not a single customer, not a single bite.

On this day the Sea of Galilee did not give up any of her fish to Simon Peter and his comrades. For a professional fisherman such a day is painful and frustrating. Bills need to be paid and families need to be fed.

Then it happened. The teacher/preacher, Jesus, came along and gave Simon an instruction that made no sense but changed this net-thrower's world.

"When He had stopped speaking, He said to Simon, 'Launch out into the deep and let down your nets for a catch.' But Simon answered and said to Him, 'Master, we have toiled all night and caught nothing; nevertheless at Your word I will let down the net.'

"And when they had done this, they caught a great number of fish, and their net was breaking. … When Simon Peter saw it, he fell down at Jesus' knees, saying, 'Depart from me, for I am a sinful man, O Lord!'

"And Jesus said to Simon, 'Do not be afraid. From now you will catch men.' So when they had brought their boats to land, they forsook all and followed Him" (Luke 5:4-6, 8, 10b).

Simon Peter knew his life was suddenly changed forever and all he could do was surrender. In awe he proclaimed, *"Depart from me for I am a sinful man, O Lord!"*

It was clear that before him stood the Son of the living God—the Deliverer for whom he had longed since childhood. He dropped to his knees knowing that he was a sinner and was standing on holy ground. His world stopped in that instant.

When Jesus said, *"Do not be afraid. From now on you will catch men,"* the trajectory of Peter's life was altered. This lowly, foul-mouthed, Galilean fisherman was transformed into a bold follower of the Christ, on his way to becoming one of the greatest voices to herald the Good News that the Kingdom of God had come to earth. He became the leader of Jesus' twelve disciples and was numbered among those of whom was said had turned the world upside down. (Acts 17:6).

The Apostle Peter was the first of the disciples to unwaveringly declare to Jesus, ***"You are the Christ, the Son of the living God"*** (Matthew 16:16). Though he faltered on the night of Jesus' arrest he went on to fearlessly preached the Gospel for the rest of his life. Around the age of sixty-five he was martyred for his faith, being crucified upside down, believing himself unworthy to die in the same manner as his Lord, right-side up.

Peter's holy moment stopped him in his tracks. An unlikely candidate to help change the world, most would never have guessed that this relatively uneducated man would author two books in the New Testament of the Bible.

Have you come to a place where you've bowed before the Son of the living God, realizing that you are a sinful man or woman? Have you been rocked by the contrast between you and the Holy One who came to save the lost?

Let's pray: *Oh God, thank You for revealing Yourself to Peter and to me. Help me to be more like Peter, walking in faith, fishing for lost souls, showing others the way to abundant life on earth and eternal life in Heaven with You. In Jesus' name we pray, amen.*

Like Peter, may we each surrender and say, "Yes," to the call to become fishers of men. If you have experienced a similar holy moment, please share your story using the hashtag, #HolyGroundAndMe

Sealed, Delivered, Changed
(Anonymous)

{Side Note: "Connie, I request that you keep this testimony anonymous or use a different name. I ask this because I haven't shared this confidential information with many people but felt led to contribute to your book."}

For my entire life, I have attended church. As a young boy, my mother regularly took me and my three siblings to church on Sunday mornings, Sunday nights, Wednesday nights, and countless revivals.

It was during those services that I began to develop a sensitivity to the Spirit of God. The Presence of the Lord leaves an impression on a person that cannot be ignored or forgotten.

Yet, though I had a sensitivity to the Spirit of God and never doubted that God was real it wasn't until I was eighteen years old that I finally decided to surrender my life to God and submit myself for His service. Looking back, I had my Damascus moment, similar to that of Saul of Tarsus.

God had opened my eyes, and I heard His voice. Yes, I heard His voice! ***"My sheep hear My voice, and I know them, and they follow Me"*** (John 10:27 KJV). I did not hear an audible voice but in my spirit, I heard Jesus calling out to me to surrender! Surrender my life, my plans, and my desires for His.

Soon after being born again, I was filled with the Holy Spirit, evidenced by speaking in tongues. (1 Corinthians 12:2-5). My heart was so on fire for God, and I had a deep desire to please Him with my life. I began to surrender the secret places of my heart and the sexual addictions that I had. Growing up I was sexually abused by a male and a female as a young boy. I was introduced to pornography by an older friend at the age of twelve, and spent six years of my life, until the age of eighteen, trying to find freedom from the chains of sexual abuse and addiction. Soon after I had surrendered to Jesus, God broke those chains and healed my heart. I had never experienced this level of freedom ever in my life. The Lord had removed all shame, guilt, and filthiness from my soul.

One night I can vividly remember having an encounter with

Jesus that I will never forget though it was thirteen years ago. It was a Friday night and the next morning I had made plans to get up around five a.m. to drive to Floyd County to help my boss pick up pigs on his livestock trailer. The reason I can remember this encounter with the Lord is that I have never had a problem sleeping past my alarm or ever missing a day of work in my life.

But that Friday night I can remember being in a deep sleep in my room when suddenly a supernatural light invaded my bedroom. It was so bright I could barely open my eyes for fear of hurting myself. Not only was this light blinding, I felt like I was under such a heavy weight, so much so that I could not even move. The light was unlike anything I had ever witnessed before, and this weight was not a suffocating weight or a weight that hurt me, but I truly believe it was the weighty glory of the Lord. I know I encountered the glory of God; the Shekinah glory had rested on me. I cannot explain this encounter other than that the awesome and mighty presence of the Lord had invaded my bedroom.

This encounter with Jesus exhausted and drained my physical body in such a way that every alarm I had set to wake up for work the next morning, I slept right through them. I also slept through every missed call from my boss and co-workers. I can still remember waking up, and thinking, how did this happen and what just happened to me. And it was later, upon meditating in God's Word and praying, that the Lord revealed that He had met with me—that He had revealed a small measure of His glory and power to me. I can't help but think of how the Angel of the Lord (Jesus, Pre-Incarnate) met with Jacob in Genesis 32.

Genesis 32:24-30: *"Then Jacob was left alone, and a Man wrestled with him until the breaking of day. Now when He saw that He did not prevail against him, He touched the socket of his hip; and the socket of Jacob's hip was out of joint as He wrestled with him. And He said, 'Let Me go, for the day breaks.' But he said, 'I will not let You go unless You bless me!' So He said to him, 'What is your name?' He said, 'Jacob.' And He said, 'Your name shall no longer be called Jacob, but Israel; for you have struggled with God and with men, and have prevailed.' Then Jacob asked, saying, 'Tell me Your name, I pray.' And He said, 'Why is it that you ask about My name?' And He blessed him there. So Jacob called the name of the place Peniel: 'For I have seen God face to face, and my life is preserved.'"*

Please don't misunderstand me, I am not calling myself Jacob or that the Lord met with me exactly in that fashion. But this I know, I encountered God in a holy and mighty way that Friday night or early Saturday morning, and my walk of faith has not been the same since.

Let's pray: *Father God, we're so grateful for Your great love and amazing grace; that You reach down and meet us where we are—whether in a pit of sin or the mire of addiction. We're never so far that You cannot reach us and free us and shine Your glorious light on us. Oh, Holy God, we thank You and praise You, for breaking the bonds of shame and guilt and carrying us into freedom and rejoicing. How can we thank You enough? All we can give You is ourselves, which is exactly what You want. Here—take me. I'm Yours. In Jesus' name, I pray, amen.*

Have you been held captive to shame and guilt because of things done to you as a child, or been in bondage to porn addiction or some other sexual sin? Has God set you free and healed you from trauma, guilt, and shame? If so, you may share your experience using the hashtag, #HolyGroundAndMe

Be Not Intimidated
(Ezekiel – Old Testament)

"So when I saw it, I fell on my face."
What had Ezekiel seen? What caused this intense reaction?

When we read the entire first chapter of The Book of Ezekiel, we get a detailed description of what Ezekiel saw. Things like a whirlwind containing a cloud of fire, a wheel within a wheel, four headed creatures with wings, and hands, and calves' feet, the noise of many waters—all this would indeed capture our attention. Words like spectacular, astonishing, and extraordinary cannot begin to describe all that God showed him that day. Yahweh had pulled back the veil allowing this man of God, a young Jewish priest, to see with spiritual eyes a most astounding sight and all he could do was fall on his face before the Holy One. Check it out for yourself by reading that chapter, imagining yourself in Ezekiel's sandals.

Then God began to instruct Ezekiel:

"So when I saw it, I fell on my face, and I heard a voice of One speaking. And He said to me, 'Son of man, stand on your feet, and I will speak to you.' Then the Spirit entered me when He spoke to me, and set me on my feet; and I heard Him who spoke to me. And He said to me: 'Son of man, I am sending you to the children of Israel, to a rebellious nation that has rebelled against Me; they and their fathers have transgressed against Me to this very day'" (Ezekiel 1:28b-2:3).

Even though Ezekiel was among those captured and deported to Babylonia, God had a work for him while in captivity. It is believed that he was about thirty-five years old at the time. God was making it clear that He was not only in Jerusalem but was with His people in Babylon as well.

Ezekiel found himself there on holy ground in a holy encounter with the God of the universe. As far as we know, he had not asked for it nor was he expecting such a thing. The Lord captivated his attention, even giving him a glimpse of the throne of God. This man of God was indeed now ready to receive his instructions.

Knowing the rebellious hearts of His people, God warned Ezekiel that they may not be receptive to His words that would be coming out of Ezekiel's mouth.

God told Ezekiel, ***"For they are impudent and stubborn children. I am sending you to them, and you shall say to them, 'Thus says the Lord GOD.' As for them, whether they hear or whether they refuse—for they are a rebellious house—yet they will know that a prophet has been among them. And you, son of man, do not be afraid of them nor be afraid of their words, though briers and thorns are with you and you dwell among scorpions; do not be afraid of their words or dismayed by their looks, though they are a rebellious house. You shall speak My words to them whether they hear or whether they refuse, for they are rebellious"*** (Ezekiel 2:4-7).

I'm (Connie) intrigued that God told Ezekiel not to be intimidated by their words nor even by their facial expressions. Several years ago, while studying The Book of Ezekiel, I was gripped by that passage. It was a life-changing moment for me. The fear of man has been and continues to be a problem for me but since the Holy Spirit highlighted that Passage for me, I've had more confidence in speaking up about Jesus and Bible truths. I haven't perfected that virtue but have significantly improved.

"The fear of man brings a snare, but whoever trusts in the Lord shall be safe" (Proverbs 29:25).

God actually gave me a vision that day as I was meditating on that Passage in Ezekiel. In my mind's eye I saw a person at the edge of Hell, like on a cliff with flaming fire below. I recognized the person in my vision, although I didn't know who they were in reality.

As they were about to step into that fiery abyss, they turned their face toward me and said, "Why didn't you tell me?" My heart sank because I knew it was too late for them and they were condemned to spend eternity in Hell. I'll never forget it.

Has the fear of man ever caused you to be hesitant to speak to someone about Jesus or about other biblical truths? What has helped you overcome those hesitations?

God knew the children of Israel were rebellious and that many would not want to hear His messages. God also knew Ezekiel and that he would be intimidated by the responses of some of the people. He warned Ezekiel and encouraged him to move forward in proclaiming the important messages He would give him. Then Ezekiel followed through.

When we read further in The Book of Ezekiel, we see the hard words that this priest/prophet brought to God's people but in the end, he prophesied that they would eventually return to their homeland, Israel, and rebuild the city of Jerusalem. When we read the books of Ezra and Nehemiah, we see the fulfilment of Ezekiel's prophesy that they did return.

Ezekiel had many holy moments with God. He endured hardships from his fellow men. Those holy moments gave him the strength to stand against the hard times and the ridicule.

Let's pray: *Father, thank You for showing us the amazing visions you gave Your servant, Ezekiel. And thank You for leading him throughout his life, giving him the words and the clarity to tell Your people messages and prophesies You wanted them to hear. As we learn from the example of Ezekiel, to not be intimidated when speaking to others about You. Help us to listen for Your words and relay them to others when You ask us to do so. We want to hear you Lord, and we want others to hear You too. Thank You, for hearing our prayer. In Jesus' name we pray, amen.*

Have you experienced a spectacular vision or encounter with God? Did He give you instructions or call you to a ministry or service? Have you ever felt intimidated when you wanted to talk to someone about the Lord? If you'd like, please share your experience using the hashtag, #HolyGroundAndMe

My Encounter with The Holy Ghost
(Yvetta)

I was raised in a small town where there were only three things to do other than go to school: 1. Attend church. 2. Go roller skating. 3. Go to the movies.

Baptized at an early age, on Sunday mornings I could be found at Sunday School and in the worship service, singing in the choir. I was a church attender who had not encountered God, Jesus, or the Holy Ghost.

As I grew older, finished school, and got married I knew something was missing in my life. I tried filling that empty space in my heart with drinking, partying, and doing drugs. I didn't know that the empty space was put there by my Creator and only He could fill it. My life was so miserable that I was contemplating suicide. I later learned that my spiritual enemy, the devil, wanted me to act on that so I would not fulfill God's purpose and calling in my life.

In 1985 I cried out to God and He led me to a church where I could learn how to live holy and not just be a churchgoer. For the first time in my life, I saw the power of God on display. The manifestation of the Gifts of The Spirit would go forth regularly. By the Spirit, the word of wisdom; the word of knowledge; faith; the gifts of healing; working of miracles; prophecy; discerning of spirits; various kinds of tongues; and the interpretation of tongues, were operating at some point in the service. I knew my newly found church family had power that I needed and thirsted for. Matthew 5:6 (KJV) states: ***"Blessed are they which do hunger and thirst after righteousness: for they shall be filled."*** I developed an appetite for the Gifts of the Spirit and became hungry and thirsty for righteousness. Praying, reading, and study the Word of God consumed my whole being.

I began attending Tuesday Night Bible study where the teacher taught about why the baptism of the Holy Ghost was an essential part of the believer's life.

After our Friday night service, we would have all night prayer from 10pm until 6am. We would tarry for the Holy Ghost at the altar. While tarrying there, several women encouraged me to believe

God that I had received the Holy Ghost by faith and begin to use my heavenly language.

I did just that and then it happened. I received by faith and began to speak in tongues as the Spirit of God gave utterance. There I was, six months pregnant with my first child (in 1986)—my daughter—having an Acts 2:4 experience: ***"And they were all filled with the Holy Ghost, and began to speak with other tongues, as the Spirit gave them utterance*** (KJV).

It was like power hit my body and a light bulb came on inside of me, lighting up my whole body beginning at my head, going down to my toes. I felt like I was floating in thin air. Then I was slain in the Spirit and landed on the floor which was like holy ground. My spirit man came alive in this holy moment! Holy, holy, holy, is the Lord God Almighty!

I knew I was born again, and that Jesus had saved me, but now my spirit man was alive. I began to see and understand things in the spiritual realm that I knew nothing about. My spiritual eyes and ears were open to the things of God. My baptism in the Holy Ghost helped me have the power to obey God because as I learned to worship Him in Spirit and in Truth, I learned how to hear His voice.

My life was changed! I had help with everyday decisions. Listen to what John 14:26 (KJV) says: ***"But the Comforter, which is the Holy Ghost, whom the Father will send in my name, he shall teach you all things, and bring all things to your remembrance, whatsoever I have said unto you."***

The Holy Ghost went to work on my behalf, teaching me how to live holy, to be obedient to the Lord, to be a proper wife, a godly mother, and a faithful servant in the Kingdom of God.

The Holy Ghost became that power source I had needed. Just think of it this way; you have the plug in your hand but if you never plug it into the power source, it's just a plug in your hand. Plug it up and watch what happens.

You are the plug, and the Holy Ghost is the power source.

Seek the Holy Ghost. HE is a life changer for the believer. Every time I needed help all I had to do was ask the Holy Ghost for directions. I no longer had to *do life* by my own instructions.

If you have not received the Baptism in the Holy Ghost, I recommend you pray this prayer:

Father, I come to you in the name of Jesus Christ, thanking You for opening my spiritual eyes to my need of the Baptism of the Holy Ghost. I ask you to reveal the power that the Baptism in the Holy Ghost gives me as a child of God. Teach me to believe that it is for me and for the church today. You have not taken your Holy Spirit away. Teach me to trust You and Your Word alone. Silence all the noise that the enemy brings and shut down and traditions that may be a part of my belief system. I ask this in Jesus' name. Amen.

Have you received the Baptism in the Holy Ghost (Holy Spirit)? Your experience may not have been as dramatic as Yvetta's and that doesn't mean it's not real. Please share your thoughts, using the hashtag, #HolyGroundAndMe

[Side Note: My (Yvetta's) prayer for you comes from Isaiah 11:2 (KJV). ***"And the spirit of the Lord shall rest upon him, the spirit of wisdom and understanding, the spirit of counsel and might, the spirit of knowledge and of the fear of the LORD."***]

Recover All
(David – Old Testament)

"Now it happened..." (Samuel 30:1a).

The torment of loss and hopelessness filled their hearts as their eyes filled with tears at the sight that lay before them. A few small pillars of smoke rose from the ruins of what was once their homes, stables, and markets.

The agonizing cries of six hundred men were all that was heard. Where were their wives? Where were their sons and daughters? Their livestock was nowhere to be seen.

Ziklag lay in ashes. The Amalekites left nothing of value and these warriors of David's army were reduced to a mass of weeping men. David's two wives and his own children were among those carried away—hostages in the hands of their enemy.

The weight of responsibility was almost more than David could bear. His precious family—gone. The anguish of his men turned to anger, and those once faithful followers now spoke of stoning their leader. He was at a loss. Everything he cared for was gone. All he had was God.

In desperation his thoughts turned to his only possibility of hope. *"And David was greatly distressed; for the people spake of stoning him, because the soul of all the people was grieved, every man for his sons and for his daughters: but David encouraged himself in the LORD his God"* (1 Samuel 30:6 KJV).

In a holy moment of mindfulness, David remembered the faithfulness of his God. He invited and allowed God to step into his pit of despair and he received strength to take the next step.

David asked the priest, Abiathar, to bring him the ephod, which is made of fine linen and gold. The woven yarns are of the colors blue, representing Heaven, purple liken to the royal priesthood, and scarlet, the color of the blood of sacrifices.

Then David prayed. He inquired of the Lord, asking what he should do. The Lord immediately answered saying to him, *"Pursue, for you shall overtake them and without fail recover all"* (1 Samuel 30:8b).

David and his men did just that. Along the way, God sent a man to show him exactly where the Amalekites were located. David and his men attacked the enemy and not a single one escaped. All the families of David and his men were recovered along with the livestock and much spoil. There was so much spoil that even after awarding portions to his men he donated some to the elders and friends throughout the region of Judah.

David and his men had fallen into deep despair when they saw they had each one lost everything. They knew their enemy would be ruthless toward their wives, sons, and daughters. It was a bad day. God heard their cries and responded to the prayer of their leader.

Have you experienced what seemed to be a total loss? Are you in a bottomless pit of despair?

Like David, remember there is a God. There is a God who sees you. He sees every detail of every situation. Remember the One who is the same today, yesterday, and every day. We may not have an ephod, but we have our Bibles containing much encouragement in Psalms, history, and miracles. It is an amazing record of God's faithfulness. Cry out to God, knowing that He hears your pleas and encourage yourself in the Lord. He is there for you every minute of every day.

When no one else is for us, God is. He knows us and is well aware of what is best for us. Plus, He can help us get to the place where we need to be. Lay it all out to Him. He's listening.

Let's pray: *Oh God, You hear my cries and You turn Your listening ear toward me. I'm so grateful for that. You always know what I should do in every situation. Help me to listen intently and hear Your voice with the answers and the encouragement I need. Thank You, wonderful Father. In Jesus' name I pray, amen.*

If you'd like to share your experience of God coming through when you were discouraged, please do so, using the hashtag, #HolyGroundAndMe

[Side Note: The thirteenth chapter of 1 Samuel begins with the words, "Now it happened" and contains many more details of this unique event in the life of David and his followers. I encourage you to check it out.]

My Jabbok Moment
(J.D. Wininger)

"And He said, 'Let me go, for the day breaks.' But he said, 'I will not let you go unless You bless me!'" (Genesis 32:26).

Many have said that the Holy Bible is the one book man can never fully understand. I agree. It's because God has proven over and over that no matter how much I study, pray, research, and meditate on His Word, I continue to find and learn new things. Something I've discovered over the past five plus decades of learning to walk with Christ is that everything God wants us to know is not written in black and white. While we find all knowledge in His Word, there are some things God wants us to work to discover. It is in this effort His lessons are best written upon our heart.

One example of learning beyond His written word is the names of God. There are many names assigned, and some (e.g., God's I AM statements) His Word has given us. Others, God compels us to discover. Elohim Shama, the God who hears, is one God showed me as I came to know Him as my Lord. He has reminded me of this name many times, through answered prayers.

Often, we think of prayer as a solemn, holy, quiet time of peaceful transcendence as we reach into Heaven. Silence all around us, heads bowed, hands folded or lifted toward Heaven. That hasn't always been the case for me. Perhaps resulting from my tumultuous childhood, my soul has an independent streak a mile wide. In the past three decades, God has slowly been shrinking it, but sometimes it still shows up. Being born with a warrior spirit served me well in the military. Fighting for every inch of ground is not always the best spirit for Christians to hold on to.

Finding salvation at fifteen, I, like many new Christians, fell into the trap of looking to man for guidance about how to be a Christian rather than God. For many years, I tried and failed at being a Christian. I can blame it on a lack of real discipleship, poor examples, and various other excuses, but at the end of the day, it came down to one thing. My refusal to surrender to God and allow Him to control, lead, and change my life. My desire to walk on both sides of my life (spiritual and carnal) led to disastrous results.

At twenty-one, I decided God needed my help, so I abandoned my boyhood prayers for a wife and rushed into marriage with a little *church girl* who caught my eye. Five years into the marriage, I realized we weren't what God wanted for the other. Ten years later, the inevitable divorce devastated me. Fallout from divorce moved me to a job halfway across the country. It seemed like I had lost everything—family, home, business, friends, and so on.

After spending my first CHRISTmas alone, with no family, friends, presents to share, or even a lighted tree, my depression found its lowest point. The endless stream of one-night stands, drinking myself to sleep each night, and being angry at the world reached a crescendo. It was during my job's shut-down period between CHRISTmas and New Year's that I decided I could not live like this any longer. I realized my choice was take my life or find my way back to God. Satan was sitting on my shoulder during this time, and his whispers grew louder and louder. "If God was so good, why did He let all these bad things happen to you? You don't need Him. He's unreliable and never gave you what He promised. You're too far gone, anyway."

Sitting at my makeshift desk, in a dreary one-bedroom apartment, I looked at a half-empty bottle of Jack Daniels with my hand on a .38-caliber revolver. The only weapon that survived my divorce. Yet something—someone—deep within me cried out, "STOP!"

"Why should I God? You didn't give me anything You promised! You didn't live up to your end of the bargain." I was determined to have it out with God. Some might think it was my biggest mistake. I look back at that moment now and consider it among my greatest blessings.

I heard the voice inside me ask, "What bargain? Show Me where I promised you a life without problems? I'm waiting." So, I ran to my closet to find the old King James Bible my ex-mother-in-law had given me the night before I moved to the Chicago area. Dusting it off, I began looking for promises I was told and believed were in the Bible, but I never looked for myself. I was frantically searching the book and my mind. Every time I attempted to share what I thought that voice chided me, "Look again, you're remembering what you don't know!" This back and forth continued into the second day. Finally, with no sleep or peace, I had had enough.

"Lord, I've prayed, gone to church, did good works in my community, and helped others. How can you abandon me after all I've done for You?" No sooner than I shouted those words, my entire body shuddered. An icy chill ran through me, followed by a warmth I had never experienced before. God no longer spoke to me but spoke through me.

His words echoed throughout my apartment. "You have done nothing for me! Yet I have used you to do my bidding, even as unwilling as you so often are. I gave you life, protected your life, and it is time for you to surrender your life to me. It's mine!" As tears flowed, I realized my time of wrestling with God had ended. While He didn't dislocate my hip and rename me Israel (as He did Jacob at the edge of the Jabbok River), He instead broke my spirit. Sitting in a pool of tears, begging His forgiveness for all my stubborn pride, God came alongside and held me close. In what I refer to as my first "Heart Hug," He turned my tears into rejoicing. I realized that for the first time in my life, I had fully surrendered to Him. That was December 1996, twenty-one years after I had asked His Son to save me. Sometimes, holy ground is found sitting at a makeshift desk in a dreary, little one-bedroom apartment on a cold and snowy winter day.

I look back upon that winter day and realize how it was all part of God's plan to bring me back to Him. Some Christians, from their moment of salvation, surrender their lives to Christ and grow to become strong, vibrant, Spirit-filled Christians, looking for every opportunity for God to use them. Others, like me, are more like an artichoke. God peels away one layer at a time until He reaches our heart and leads us to surrender to His will.

Since God came near, He has remained my patient and steady friend—guiding me, sometimes ever so slowly, into a right and productive life of service to Him. My full and complete surrender to Him didn't mean Satan never tempted me or I would never experience God's trials again. It meant I would always remember to look to Him during those times. In the years since, God has put me back on His path for my life and He continues to prune, groom, and grow me for His service.

It was just a few months after my "Jacob's Jabbok Moment" (Genesis 32:22-32), that God brought the woman who would become my life partner into my world. Beautiful, funny, intelligent, and patient, she was more than I had dared to pray for. Not long after we had met, I penned *God's Gift*, a poem, to memorialize His answer to long ago petitions. I had long forgotten those prayers for a forever wife, yet God reminded me He is Elohim Shama, the God who hears.

In reflecting upon God's working in my life, I can see where His presence and protection has blessed me, even long before I knew Him as my Savior and Lord. I learned that while He may have been my Savior, He would not be satisfied until I made Him Lord over my life.

It's interesting how the Hebrew word Jabbok means "emptying". That's exactly what God did to me in my Jabbok moment. He emptied me of the world that entangled my soul and brought me into alignment with His will—putting me back on the path of His plan and my destiny.

In the years since I surrendered to God and made Him Lord over my life, He has blessed me more than I could ever hope for or deserve. He continues to hear and answer my prayers. It isn't always the answer I want, but the answer He deems best for my life. Learning to accept that—knowing through faith that He will work all things for good—is a sure sign of His continuing sanctification at work in my life. I can look forward to tomorrow with a faith-filled heart, resting in the knowledge that Elohim Shama is the *God Who Hears*. He listens and works in my life and others', answering my petitions when they align with His plan for my life—to bring Him glory, honor, and praise.

Let's pray: *Abba, Father, I thank You for Your steadfast desire to bring me into Your plan for my life. Your relentless pursuit, even when as the Apostle Paul said, "I was the chief sinner", shows me Your immense love for me. I pray for Your help to live a life worthy of the love, mercy, and grace You so freely give to me. Help me surrender each day to Your will for my life, so I might one day hear You say, "Well done, good and faithful servant." In Jesus' precious and holy name, I pray. Amen.*

Have you had a Jabbok Moment when you wrestled with God? What was the outcome for you? Feel free to comment on social media, using the hashtag, #HolyGroundAndMe

Okay, We've Got This
(Elisha & His Servant – Old Testament)

It was around 850 B.C., and the king of Syria was an annoyance and a threat to Israel. And it happened that somehow the king of Israel kept being informed of the movements of the Syrian army. The Syrian king was puzzled by just how those Jews kept knowing his strategies in advance.

But a servant of the Syrian king was aware of how that was happening:

"And one of his servants said, 'None, my lord, O king: but Elisha, the prophet who is in Israel, tells the king of Israel the words that you speak in your bedroom.' So he said, 'Go and spy where he is, that I may send and get him.' And it was told him, saying 'Surely, he is in Dothan'" (2 Kings 6:12-13).

So, the king of Syria sent a large army with horses and chariots to fetch Elisha. By night they surrounded the city.

Elisha's servant rose early in the morning and when he stepped outside the house he saw the vast army. He was terrified and went back in and said to Elisha, "Alas, my master, what on earth shall we do?!"

Elisha replied, "Do not fear. Those who are with us are more and mightier than those who are with them."

"And Elisha prayed, and said, 'LORD, I pray, open his eyes that he may see.' Then the LORD opened the eyes of the young man, and he saw. And behold, the mountain was full of horses and chariots of fire all around Elisha" (2 Kings 6:17).

Then the servant could see! In this incredible holy moment Elisha's servant saw the whole truth of their situation. What appeared to be dire and potentially disastrous was suddenly turned around. The young man looked around and saw God's army—an angelic host. Can you imagine a vast army with chariots of fire manned by mighty angels?

The terror that had gripped him was turned into reassurance. He could now say with confidence, "Okay, we've got this."

The plans of the Syrian king were completely flipped that day. Elisha and his servant were safe, and the threat of Syria over Israel was foiled. Elisha knew his God and the servant was learning a lesson that we would do well to remember every day.

"What shall we then say to these things? If God be for us, who can be against us?" (Romans 8:31 KJV).

On occasion, God opens the eyes of His children allowing them to see behind the thin veil that is between the natural world and the spiritual realm. This story reminds us that the spiritual realm is greater than the natural realm. This world will eventually pass away but the spiritual is eternal.

Let's pray: *Oh, Lord, help me to always remember that when I walk in faith in Christ, trusting You, we are a majority no matter what surrounds me. I want to always have confidence that You are mightier than any fear or evil that is thrown against me. And help me to always remember that You said, "Ye are of God, little children, and have overcome them: because greater is he that is in you, than he that is in the world" (1 John 4:4 KJV). Thank You, Lord. In Jesus' name I pray, amen.*

Have you been in a terrifying situation, surrounded by something mightier than you but then realized that with God you had a majority? Tell us about it, using the hashtag, #HolyGroundAndMe.

Alive and Awake
(Marla Thompson)

Holy Spirit called it "supernatural surgery" and it certainly was. Leading up to December 31, 2016 - January 1, 2017, I had lived a life that to the observer appeared lovely, settled, comfortable and happy. The hidden truth was quite different. I must briefly tell of a supernatural event in 1983, that you would think would set everything right in my life. That was not the case; I still struggled with depression and identity. However, that event did settle in my soul a covenant with God that I would never try to take my own life again. That covenant decision is what got me to 2017. The 1983 event was an anchor keeping me alive in the storms to come. God's ways are truly not our ways.

In 1983 in the darkest depression you can imagine, I could not even see light, I sought to take my own life. On a moonless night at 2 a.m. I walked into the ocean at Myrtle Beach, SC with the conclusion I would walk until I could not touch the ground, float until I became too heavy and sink in the water to finally be relieved of my darkness. I floated quite a way out into the deep. In the instant I knew I was done, only by the breath of Holy Spirit with me, I whispered "If you are who you say you are, show me right now." In an instant I was standing on the shore and light shone all around me. It was still 2 a.m. by my watch. God literally plucked me out of the sea and His Light shone all around me. I knew God was real, powerful and with me. I told Him I would never attempt to take my own life again. I knew I was making a covenant with God. He saved me from death; I would not take dying into my own hands ever again.

The supernatural encounter I had with Holy Spirit in 2017 changed EVERYTHING in my life. I knew God is who He says He is, but who does He say He is? I realized I really didn't know. I had religion's version, but religion had failed me. I was not aligned with God's true nature and character to the point of intimacy and Knowing Him and therefore I was not aligned with my own identity. So, I was always fighting for my identity as God designed me in every circumstance of life (in marriage, as a parent, at work, church, everywhere). Of course, I had moments of revelation but there was always something BIG missing in my soul and spirit. Anger, frustration, manipulation, control, sadness, despair at times were all still in the mix.

At the end of 2016 I felt I was very close to where I had been in 1983 with the exception, I wanted to die but knew I could not just check out because I told God I wouldn't. I had descended into a comatose state of mind, going through the motions but feeling nothing unless it was despair. To avoid the despair, I willed myself to live numb. For over five years I had driven the LA Freeways on my long commutes to work, daydreaming about a catastrophic wreck that would take my life and always thinking, "Oh, what a relief that would be."

On the night of December 31, 2016, I went to bed in my usual comatose state. Yet, again, in a moment, I spoke to God. This time it was, "I know You are real, but what difference does it make." I had a feeling of hopelessness. I had lost faith in everyone and everything …. except God. Even with my despairing declaration, still, the One I spoke to about my despair and hopelessness was God. He was the only one I had any hope and faith in even if it was tiny, and if He didn't make a difference, I knew I would remain comatose until I died one day.

On the morning of January 1, 2017, I awakened from sleep and instantaneously was fully awake. I sat up in the bed and looked around. I recognized the room, but everything was different. Everything was bright and light and happy. I was happy. I felt like an entirely brand-new person. I could feel my eyes were wide and with laughter I spoke out loud, "What happened?!" I clearly heard Holy Spirit say, "We performed supernatural surgery on you during the night."

That entire day Holy Spirit talked with me like you talk with a dear intimate friend. All day we talked. Holy Spirit told me all about Papa God (He was re-introduced to me that day as Papa), Jesus my brother and friend, and Himself my Spirit guide. He told me all about myself. Holy Spirit told me I had been restored to youth, to the place where my spiritual gifts were oppressed, returned to the energy, zeal and purpose God put in me before the beginning of time. Nothing was lost. He told me I am created to create, and art would be a vehicle for me to fulfill my Kingdom assignment. As a child I loved to draw but by the time I graduated from college I was convinced I was NOT an artist and had laid down all creating. I had not really drawn or painted for over 30 years.

God told me that my inheritance is like that of Caleb: *"But my servant Caleb—this is a different story. He has a different spirit; he follows me passionately. I'll bring him into the land that he scouted and his children will inherit it"* (Numbers 14:24 TPT).

Holy Spirit asked me if I would give up my life and follow Jesus into the unknown? I said, "YES." I KNEW I had been transformed in a day. And from then on, my YES became an anchor because Papa, Jesus, and Holy Spirit have indeed turned my life upside down. Because people have free will and others chose not to go with me where Jesus led me, a marriage that had been broken decades earlier now ended. I left my corporate job of thirty-one years to be an artist.

Another anchor verse God gave me is Joshua 1:9 NLT: *"This is my command—'be strong and courageous! Do not be afraid or discouraged. For the Lord your God is with you wherever you go.'"*

Every day in 2017 I was on my face before God eating and drinking His Word. All of 2018 God sent me on prayer drives up the western coast to experience His Love and visions for a coming time. In 2019 I received the instruction to sell my possessions and begin a prayer drive with no ending in sight. I lived on the road, from my car, September 2019 until the summer of 2021.

In 2021 God gave me a landing place, for a season only, to explore art and bring Light and Salt to emerging Ekklesia hubs. Today, I am parked in Fancy Gap, VA and travel out every week to spread the good news of the Kingdom sharing the revelations I receive from God for these days. I can clearly see how everything I survived 1983 through 2017 was necessary for me to now thrive in my identity as a Child of God advancing His Kingdom in such a time as this. I am alive and fully awake.

Join with me and let's declare this, another anchor passage: *"This forever-song I sing of the gentle love of God! Young and old alike will hear about your faithful, steadfast love—never failing!"* (Psalm 89:1 TPT).

Let's pray: *Thank You, Papa God for Your great love and Your watch care over us even when we sink beneath Your design for us. Your eyes never turn from us and Your reach is never too far to lift us up and wake us up. Help us now to embrace the divine identity You gave each one of us and to walk in the calling of Your Abba's heart. With the help of Holy Spirit we can do this for Your glory and for our own good. In Jesus' name we pray, amen.*

Marla D Thompson, www.fiercebirdstudio.com, Fancy Gap, VA

Have you strayed from the identity God gave you? Have you felt discouraged and didn't want to go on? Would you like us to pray for you? Please share your thoughts using the hashtag, #HolyGroundAndMe

Who Are You, Lord?
(Saul/Paul – New Testament)

"Who are You, Lord?" Saul cried out in desperation.

Helpless on the ground and blinded by the sudden bright light, this proud Jewish man could not fathom what was happening.

The voice had called him by name saying, ***"Saul, Saul, why are you persecuting Me?"*** (Acts 9:4b).

He had Saul's undivided attention and identified Himself: ***"'I am Jesus, whom you are persecuting. It is hard for you to kick against the goads.' So he (Saul), trembling and astonished, said, 'Lord, what do You want me to do?' Then the Lord said to him, 'Arise and go into the city, and you will be told what you must do'"*** (Acts 9:5b-6).

Still blinded, Saul's companions led him into the city of Damascus where God had prepared for his next steps and his life calling to be revealed.

Meanwhile, in the city, Saul's divine appointment was already arranged. A certain follower of Jesus, named Ananias, heard the voice of the Lord in a vision: ***"So the Lord said to him, 'Arise and go to the street called Straight, and inquire at the house of Judas for one called Saul of Tarsus, for behold he is praying. And in a vision he has seen a man named Ananias coming in and putting his hand on him, so that he might receive his sight'"*** (Acts 9:11-12).

Now, Ananias was a bit reluctant, for news had preceded Saul that he was traveling to Damascus for the purpose of locating followers of Jesus and dragging them back to Jerusalem to be imprisoned by the religious leaders. Saul even had documents from those leaders authorizing his mission.

The Lord said to Ananias, ***"'Go, for he is a chosen vessel of Mine to bear My name before Gentiles, kings, and the children of Israel. For I will show him how many things he must suffer for My name's sake. And Ananias went his way and entered the house; and laying his hands on him he said, 'Brother Saul, the Lord Jesus, who appeared to you on the road as you came, has*** *sent me that you may receive your sight and be filled with the Holy Spirit.' Immediately there fell from his eyes something like scales, and he received his sight at once; and he arose and was baptized"* (Acts 9:15-18).

This is a true account of a man on a road of destruction who is arrested by Jesus in a blinding light. The temple veil had been torn and Saul, who was later called Paul, was beyond the veil and in the holy presence of the Light of the world. Suddenly, in a most frightening way he fell at the feet of the Christ onto holy ground.

The trajectory of his life was reversed. In the presence of the Son of God, Saul heard with spiritual ears and then could see with spiritual vision his purpose and calling. Known to us as Paul, he played a major role in turning the world upside down. (Acts 17:6). We too have a role to play in turning our world upside down by shining the light of Christ into dark places.

Let's pray: *Oh Lord, Your amazing transformation of Paul is an incredible testimony for us to see what You can do with one man. Thank You for what You have done through Paul to change his world and to write much of the Bible whose writings help us learn to be transformed into holy vessels for Your use in the building of Your eternal kingdom. We want to yield to Your plan. Help us, Lord. In Jesus' name we pray, amen.*

Have you experienced a "Damascus Road" type of encounter in which God stopped you in your tracks and reversed the direction of your life? If so, please share using the hashtag, #HolyGroundAndMe

Jesus and Me
(Ginny Ailine Perfater)

I've been walking with the Lord for sixteen years and have had many encounters with Him. He has given me numerous dreams and visions along the way. As I've drawn closer to Him and have been sanctified by His Holy Spirt, He has shared great things with me. Since 2020, the number of dreams and visions the Lord has given me has increased dramatically!

Just before the Feast of Trumpets in 2023 the Lord gave me a vision. This was not a vision I wanted. It was terrible. I saw Hell. I saw a gathering of demons. In front of the demons stood Satan. He was at a podium and as he spoke the demons were getting more and more excited. Then Satan began to grow. He was getting bigger and bigger. I cried out to the Lord, "No, I don't want to be here." He said to me, "You're not there. I am only allowing you to see it, to warn you." I knew immediately that it was going to look like Satan was winning. That it would look like he was growing in great power and authority and that I must prepare myself for times of great evil ahead.

The next night, as a lay in bed saying my prayers, I asked God to reveal anything to me that He'd like. Then suddenly, I remembered my vision from the night before, and I made a request. I said, "Lord, please give me something to hope for, for You always give me the warnings and tonight I need something to hope for." As I slept that night, I dreamt that I was flying over a new earth with the Lord. The old had passed away and there was a beautiful green mountain and a river flowing from it. The river was winding through the forest. It looked perfect and untouched by man. It was glorious. It gave me immense peace and joy. I knew in my spirit that God is restoring His creation. I knew that once again His creation would be pure, peaceful, and beautiful. I knew that we would have perfect union with the Lord again, like in the Garden of Eden, and that we would be with Him as He had intended from the beginning. It is coming! We are in but the birthing pains.

I've had visions of the great battles that will take place towards the end of days. I have seen terrible things happening in America, but I have also seen stadiums filled with people worshiping the Lord. As I ponder all these things, nothing I have seen changed my life like an encounter I had with Him about sixteen years ago.

I was raised in a poor family in the New River Valley, of Virginia, located in the heart of Appalachia. My grandfather built a home where many of us lived through the years. At one time, nineteen of us lived in that home. My family was close. We helped each other, but we were very dysfunctional. There were things we just didn't talk about in that home, and Jesus was one of them. I never heard His name, read the Bible, or prayed with my family. We didn't say, "I love you," or show affection in any way. However, I always knew there was a God who created everything and everyone, and I prayed to Him every night. I prayed for everyone in my family, for everyone at school, and for people all over the world. I would pray for hours in my bed, just me and the Lord.

When I was nine years old, Mr. Doug came walking through the low-income apartment complex where I was staying the night with my cousins. He took me and a group of kids to a little building around the corner, and he began to teach us about Jesus. At the end of his lesson, he gave an alter call. The Lord was calling me up, but I was too scared to move. As I wrestled with the Holy Spirit, Mr. Doug pointed at me and waved me to the front. I looked beside me and behind me, terrified that he had noticed me, but he had! Before I knew it, my legs were carrying me to the front of that little building, and I was giving my life to the Lord. The Holy Spirit filled me, and I fell back into the arms of a young man who was behind me. I was different, and now I had a name to call out to when I prayed. His name is Jesus.

Although I was different, my family life wasn't. I went back to that home—back to no affection and back to no understanding of Jesus. I spent a lot of time alone.

When I got to high school, I met a boy and began living in sin. I knew deep down it was wrong, but desperately wanted love and affection. We dated for eight years. During my senior year of high school, I got pregnant, and my boyfriend began to spiral downhill. My pregnancy and a football injury led him to seek comfort in drugs, which ultimately led to our breakup a few years later.

During my pregnancy, my family lost our home. Before I knew

it, I was a single mom—broke, broken, and desperate. My daughter and I got a low-income apartment, and I went back to college and got a job. But the more money I made the more our housing costs increased. After finishing my associate's degree, I had to take a break from college so that I could work more to pay our rent. When my uncle asked me to move in his home and take care of my grandfather, I was delighted. This was a win-win. I would only have to pay utilities and cook and clean for my grandad. This would allow me to go back and finish my education. Things were looking up, and I was so excited. Only three months into our arrangement, my uncle needed to move back home. That meant I had to find another place to live. Having given up my apartment, I had no where to go. My only choice was to move back in with my mom and stepdad.

This was not something I wanted to do. I'd hit rock bottom. Nothing was working out, and I desperately wanted stability for my daughter. That's when I called out to the Lord. I'll never forget that night. I was in my car, on my way to their house. I had just finished loading the last of our things into a storage unit. My daughter, who was three years old by then, was asleep, hunched over in her car seat. I turned on the radio and heard a song, titled, "Lay 'Em Down," by a band called "NEEDTOBREATHE."

The song talks about how we can lay all our troubles down and just give them to the Lord. All our sins and weaknesses, whether we're rich or poor; if we're lost and lonely; broken and hurting—we can lay it all down. Our Heavenly Father can carry all our burdens. I was desperate and overwhelmed. The words resonated in my spirit like nothing I'd ever experienced.

As I listened to the words of this song, the Holy Spirit filled my car with His presence. Like a light shining in the darkness the Lord beckoned me back to His loving arms. I knew in an instant all the things I'd been doing wrong. I knew that I'd been looking for love in all the wrong places; that nothing, other than God could fill the emptiness inside of me. So, I gave it all to Him! I fell deeply in love with Jesus on that holy night in that holy place. My car became holy ground where God met with me and gave me hope and a future. Suddenly, the stars were shining brighter than I'd ever seen before.

The next day the grass was greener, the trees were fuller, the river shimmered in the sun in a way I'd never noticed. The colors seemed more vibrant. The love of the Lord changed everything for me, in an instant. What was my darkest, most difficult moment, became the most beautiful time of my life. I read the Bible. I studied. I prayed. I began to attend church. I turned from my sin as God began to reveal more and more that I needed to let go of, and my whole life began to change. I knew that my daughter and I were going to be fine because God loved us and was leading us. It was like He was holding us in His hands.

In his psalm, King David expressed much of what I was experiencing: *"Hear, O LORD, when I cry with my voice! Have mercy also upon me, and answer me. When You said, 'Seek My face, my heart said to You, 'Your face, LORD, I will seek.' … When my father and my mother forsake me, then the LORD will take care of me. Teach me Your way, O LORD, and lead me in a smooth path"* (Psalm 27:7-11a).

I've been walking with the Lord now for sixteen years. I speak to Him every day all the time, and He leads me and guides me daily. Sixteen years of His faithfulness. He is still giving me what I need. He is still revealing areas in my life where I need to do better. He takes me by the hand and leads me closer to Himself. It is the most important and beautiful relationship I have ever had! I have a love I never imagined possible with the Creator of the universe. I still relish in the beauty of His craftsmanship. Everything He made is beautiful and draws me into a deeper revelation of Him. Whether it is the pink and golden hues of a sunset, or the way the wind rustles the leaves of the trees on an early autumn day, or the way mountains rise to the heavens and fall into the valleys, I'm captivated by the wonder of my God. It all reminds me of His great love for me. He loves me and I love Him.

Let's Pray: *Oh, Abba Father, thank You for the wondrous love you have for me. It is unconditional and beyond anything I could have hoped for. I'm so grateful that You have rescued me from myself and my sins and that You're working in the life and future of my precious daughter. By Your Holy Spirit, help me to walk in Your ways and do Kingdom work according to Your divine plan. In Jesus' wonderful name, amen.*

Has the Lord rescued you from yourself or from a bad situation? Have you returned home to God and the security of His love after a period of time trying to do things your own way? Please share your thoughts, using the hashtag, #HolyGroundAndMe

Meeting on the Mountain
(Jesus, Peter, John, James – New Testament)

"Then it happened, as they were parting from Him, that Peter said to Jesus, 'Master, it is good for us to be here; and let us make three tabernacles: one for You, one for Moses and one for Elijah'—not knowing what he said" (Luke 9:33).

This enthusiastic, impulsive Peter wanted to jump into action to commemorate the amazing event he, James, and John had just witnessed. But God Himself came on the scene interrupting Peter, essentially saying "Be quiet and listen." No monuments were to be erected.

"While he (Peter) *was still speaking, behold, a bright cloud overshadowed them; and suddenly a voice came out of the cloud, saying, 'This is My beloved Son, in whom I am well pleased. Hear Him!' And when the disciples heard it, they fell on their faces and were greatly afraid. But Jesus came and touched them and said, 'Arise, and do not be afraid.' When they had lifted up their eyes, they saw no one but Jesus only. Now as they came down from the mountain, Jesus commanded them, saying, 'Tell the vision to no one until the Son of Man is risen from the dead'"* (Matthew 17:5-9).

Peter, James, and John, known as Christ's inner circle, had just witnessed a most amazing event and then realized they were on holy ground when Yahweh put them in their place: *"They fell on their faces and were greatly afraid."*

They had had been overcome by the presence of God when enveloped in the glory cloud from on high. What was it they had observed that day?

Luke records it: Jesus *"took Peter, John, and James and went up on the mountain to pray. As He prayed, the appearance of His face was altered, and His robe became white and glistening. And behold, two men talked with Him, who were Moses and Elijah, who appeared in glory and spoke of His decease* (departure) *which He was about to accomplish at Jerusalem"* (Luke 9:28b-31).

Matthew describes it: *"and He was transfigured before them.*

His face shown like the sun, and His clothes became as white as the light. And behold, Moses and Elijah appeared to them, talking with Him" (Matthew 17:2-3).

Nothing Peter could say nor monuments he could build were fitting in that moment. God ordained that these three disciples observe the meeting on the mountain. The brilliance of Jesus' face and clothes; the presence of the great patriarchs, Moses, representing the Law, and Elijah, representing the prophets, was not mere sensory overload. It was a holy moment on holy ground with the exclamation point of God's own voice.

How does a person contain such things?

How does the human brain process such a supernatural cosmic occurrence?

Peter's attempt landed him and the other two face down on the ground under the glorious presence of God. Jesus relieved their fear and told them to tell no one of their experience until after He had risen from the dead.

Have you had an encounter with God that put you on the ground or on the floor? I haven't experienced that, but I've seen it happen to others.

Have you heard the audible voice of God? I haven't heard His voice audibly but many times I've clearly heard His voice speak to my spirit. That usually happens when I'm reading or meditating on Scripture.

If you've had this type of experience, did you tell others immediately? Why do you think Jesus didn't want this event told until after His resurrection?

After my experience with the mighty rushing wind many years went by before I shared about it. I was so overwhelmed that such a thrilling thing could happen to me, and I knew I couldn't explain it in mere words that could do it justice. I didn't know something like that could happen to an ordinary person like me. Being raised in a traditional church I was unaware of manifestations of God's Spirit or His holy presence in such a tangible way in modern days.

Let's pray: *Oh Father, what an incredible encounter You gave those three disciples. Thank You for showing it to us in Your Word. Help us to be open and to yearn for more of You—for more of Your holy presence in our own lives. You are a wondrous and glorious God, and we want all You wish for us to have and experience. In Jesus' name we pray, amen.*

If you have experienced anything like what Peter, James, and John did, please share about it using the hashtag, #HolyGroundandMe

My Life, His Story
(Lisa)

God has stepped in and helped create many stories and testimonies throughout my life. As they unfolded a book of my life began to form.

I could go back and share the story of being sexually abused at age five. I could share the story of my brother attempting suicide, almost dying in front of our family. I could share the story of being poor and having no running water in our home while growing up, or when my marriage was on the rocks. I could explain how it was growing up with a dad, who was what we called a "dry drunk."

I would then have to take you on the journey of how God stepped into each of those stories, and healed, saved, mended relationships; how chains were broken, and bondages were loosed. I could share many personal stories of God's goodness, grace, healing and mercy and how He stood by His promises each and every day.

The story that I am sharing now is the most recent. I want NO honor or eyes on me, but I am here to give glory to God, because without Him and the Holy Spirit living in me, I truly would not be here today. Revelation 12:11 tells us that we have defeated the enemy, by the blood of the Lamb and by the word of our testimony. We claim victory.

So, let me tell you about my Jesus and how the Holy Spirit showed up in a mighty way to comfort me through this battle!

On August 23, 2022, I went into Anne Arundel Medical Hospital in Maryland for surgery on my upper and lower jaw, due to deficient bone growth on each side and jawline. Because of this the jawline was not supporting my cheekbones and muscles correctly, resulting in severe pain when eating, sleeping, and talking. This was a major surgery. The recovery period was expected to be a month, with a full recovery within two months.

On August 28th I told my husband I was not feeling well. The right side of my face was hot to the touch and my face had swollen at least two times its size. We called the doctor and back to Maryland we went. By the way, the hospital is a five-hour drive from our home in Virginia.

I had developed a bone infection. They took a biopsy to find out what kind of infection we were dealing with, which takes ten days to cultivate. I spent three days going back and forth between a hotel and the surgeon's office getting IV (intravenous) antibiotics.

On Wednesday, August 31st they discovered the infection had spread to my temple. I was admitted to the hospital awaiting a CT scan to see if it was traveling to my brain. We were still waiting to hear what type of infection it was, and how it should be treated.

We had no idea that I would be admitted to the hospital therefore, my husband and I had no clothes or personal belongings. As he made the journey home, I made a separate journey.

As I lay in that hospital bed, I could have felt hopeless. I could have felt alone. I could have had self-pity. In my condition, I could not talk, and my daily thought process was foggy due to the medicine. Realizing the devil was trying to take my voice, I decided to do what I could do. I knew my God. He had come through for me and my family in the past. I may have been in a hospital bed but for me it was holy ground—a place to meet with my Creator I knew I could trust.

I made the decision to give Him all my praise. Hebrews 13:15 (NIV) came to mind: ***"Through Jesus, therefore, let us continually offer to God a sacrifice of praise—the fruit of lips that openly profess His name."***

I began making a playlist and named it "God's Got a Plan." I added songs of His faithfulness, healing, goodness, and blessings. As I lay there praising Him, the Holy Spirit filled the hospital room, and in that holy moment, in my spirit, I heard God say, "Lean into Me, and do not do things in your own strength. Do not try to write your story. I am writing it for you, and I am not finished yet, and where your voice is trying to be taken, it will be heard!"

These scriptures came to mind:

Romans 8:28, tells us that all things work together for the good to those who love God, and who are called to His purpose.

Philippians 4:13 tells us we can do all things through Christ who strengthens us.

Proverbs 3:5-6: *"Trust in the Lord with all your heart, and lean not on your own understanding; In all your ways acknowledge Him and He will direct your paths."*

I just laid there with tears streaming down my face praising my Lord, thanking the Holy Spirit, and claiming the victory that He was not done with me yet. This was a precious and holy time with my God. I felt physically helpless, but I knew where my help was coming from.

The next day, the CT scan came back negative, and the infection was not in my brain. I was going home, but this journey was not over.

Having developed another infection, I again traveled back to Maryland in October 2022. This time on the left side, the bone was growing toward the outside of my jaw. It immediately had to be removed along with the plates which had been placed in at the time of surgery, because they were holding infection.

Back on antibiotics, we waited for it to clear before planning the next steps. Then in November at my follow up appointment, we discovered the bone was still not healing. On December 3rd I went in for another surgery to clean up the remaining infection and to wire my mouth closed for eight weeks hoping it would act as a cast and allow the bone to heal.

When I returned on January 23rd, 2023, we learned that the wires did not work. I was going in for yet another surgery on January 30th.

Keep in mind that since August of 2022 the only thing I had eaten was food puréed or protein shakes which I could drink through a straw.

I was discouraged. I was disheartened. I was tired and battle-weary. Not only was it a physical battle and a battle of the mind, but it was a spiritual battle. I could see that it was a battle between the devil's plan and God's promises. The devil was whispering, "You will never get better and never speak right again." Then I heard God gently remind me: "I am Jehovah Rapha, Jehovah Jireh, I will not leave you nor forsake you." He spoke Isaiah 40:31: *"Those who hope in the Lord will renew their strength. They will soar on wings like eagles; they will run and not grow weary, they will walk and not be faint"* (NIV). And He said, "Your voice will be heard. I am not through writing your story!" I was confident that I had heard from God.

So again, I turned to praise music. I heard a song by Shane & Shane called, "You've Already Won." It talks about how no matter what comes our way God will help us overcome because He has already won.

I was learning that faith has growing pains, and it stretches you. I was learning that healing comes in different ways, and God's strength was weaving itself into every fiber of my body. No matter what battle I may be fighting He has already won. By, holding on to His promises, I knew I would come through this stronger and more assured of what God had in store for me!

On January 23rd, 2023, I returned to my doctor for what we prayed would be my final surgery. It was a ten-hour surgery. They took bone out of my hip and placed it in my jaw. After being released from the hospital, I was readmitted within a week with yet another infection. It was life threatening. On February 22nd, 2023, a drainage tube was placed in my neck and a pic line was installed.

When released to go home, I had to rely on home health, friends, and family to administer antibiotics to me daily. This was humbling, yet a reminder that I needed to lean into Him and that the battle was His.

Finally, on April 7th the pic line was removed. The bone was healing. Several setbacks and more minor surgeries followed. Then in February 2024 I had my final surgery.

Through all of this I know **His promises stand true always!**

You see, when God, stepped into my story, He knew the desires of my heart. He knew exactly what my voice was to be used for! As I have leaned into Him and let Him write this story, His promises have emerged into a new chapter in my book of life—the chapter of a ministry being birthed. With God at the helm, and me using my voice as His tool, Restoration for Women Ministry, is being used to help women heal, overcome challenges, reclaim their identity, and walk in freedom, leading them on a journey towards emerging and soaring in Jesus Christ.

SO, yes, the devil had a plan. He tried to take the voice that would minister to many women. But God had THE plan—to give me a story telling of His great promises and His great victory.

No matter what battle I may be fighting, I always remember, He is the author of my story, and in the end… He has already won!

Stand strong friends, He is not finished yet!

Let's pray: Wonderful Heavenly Father, thank You for having a plan—a story—for each of us. We are confident that Your plan is always best. Help us to trust You to weave your plan throughout our lives, knowing that the outcome will be good for us and for others as well. Thank You for giving us Your Word and Your Spirit to help us and encourage us along the way. In Jesus' name we pray, amen.

Have you experienced a medical crisis and been desperate for God to step in? If so, how did it affect you and your family? Did you trust God from the start, or did He lead you through a process of trust? Is God writing your story? Did He intervene in your trauma and let you know that your story isn't over? If you would like, please share your experience on social media using the hashtag #HolyGroundAndMe

Lisa at Restoration for Women Ministry,

www.emergeandsoar.com

You can find us on Facebook and Instagram.

Three Strikes! You're NOT Out
(Woman at the Well - New Testament)

He needed to go this route. He was compelled, even constrained in His Spirit to travel this way. His companions didn't like this route because they didn't care for the mixed-race residents. But on this day, they had no choice as they continued following Jesus.

John 4:3-6 tells us, ***"He*** [Jesus] ***left Judea and departed again to Galilee. But He needed to go through Samaria.*** (The King James Version says, ***"And He must needs go through Samaria."*** v.4) ***"So He came to a city of Samaria which is called Sychar, near the plot of ground that Jacob gave to his son Joseph. Now Jacob's well was there. Jesus therefore being wearied from His journey, sat thus by the well. It was about the sixth hour."***

It was around noon and His disciples had gone into town to buy food. When a woman from the city approached, to draw water, ***"Jesus said to her, 'Give Me a drink'"*** (v. 7b). Being a woman—a Samaritan woman at that—she replied, ***"'How is it that You, being a Jew, ask a drink from me, a Samaritan woman?' for Jews have no dealings with Samaritans.***

"Jesus answered and said to her, 'If you knew the gift of God, and who it is who says to you, 'give Me a drink,' you would have asked Him, and He would have given you living water.' ... 'Where then do You get that living water?'" she asked. (John 4:9b-11)

Jesus answered, ***"Whoever drinks of this water will thirst again, but whoever drinks of the water that I shall give him will never thirst. But the water that I shall give him will become in him a fountain of water springing up into everlasting life"*** (John 4:13b-14).

She wanted that water. He told her to go get her husband.

"I have no husband," was her reply.

Then it happened.

Jesus stunned her, saying, ***"You have well said, 'I have no husband,' for you have had five husbands, and the one whom you*** *now have now is not your husband; in that you spoke truly"* (John 4:17b-18).

"The woman said to Him, 'I know that Messiah is coming' (who is called Christ). 'When He comes, He will tell us all things.'

"Jesus said to her, 'I who speaks to you am He'" (John 4:25-26).

In that holy moment this outcast woman realized she was talking with the Son of the Living God. With three strikes against her she was still not out. A Jewish man does not associate with a woman (strike 1); especially not a woman with a bad reputation (strike 2); and Jews did not associate with Samaritans (strike 3).

Jesus has come to give living water—eternal life—to anyone who will believe. To this seemingly unqualified woman, He offered it and even revealed to her that He is the One who had been anticipated by the Jews for hundreds of years.

Many Bible scholars say that this Samaritan woman was the first person to whom He revealed His identity and that she was the first evangelist. Straight away, she dropped her waterpot and went into the city to tell others. People came out to see this Man she spoke of.

"And many of the Samaritans of that city believed in Him because of the word of the woman who testifies, 'He told me all that I ever did.' … And many more believed in Him because of His own word. Then they said to the woman, 'Now we believe, not because of what you said, for we ourselves have heard Him and we know that this is indeed the Christ, the Savior of the world'" (John 4:39, 41-42).

We don't even know her name, but this woman's life was changed forever as were the others in Sychar who believed in Jesus. When she went to draw water that day, she had no idea she would be treading on holy ground in the presence of the Son of Man, Son of God. She certainly got more than she expected.

Let's pray: Thank You, Father, that You love the outcast and those with bad reputations just as much as you love the sweetest saint. Thank You for going out of Your way to seek and save those who are lost. Your love and grace and mercy are beyond our comprehension. Help us to love and extend grace to others regardless of societal standing and declare that you are the Christ, the Son of the Living God. In Jesus' name, amen.

Were you or are you an outcast trying to find your place in this world? Have you been considered one whose reputation would not be accepted in Christian circles? Father God loves and wants every human in His family, no matter their ethnicity, social standing, or past. Whosoever believes in Him is welcome (John 3:16). Please share your comments using the hashtag, #HolyGroundAndMe

His Fullness
(Verna)

"And of his fullness we have all received, and grace for grace" (John 1:16 KJV).

In the spring of 1962, I remember my mother calling me and asking for a ride to a charismatic prayer meeting that was being held in a convent. I had heard of this movement and out of curiosity I told her I would take her. My mother was a very religious, catholic woman but had never obtained a driver's license and was dependent upon me, her oldest daughter, for rides. I tried to accommodate her as best I could.

Upon arriving at this meeting, there was a man there who had already started talking. We walked in and took our seats. Before this, most of the teaching and preaching I had heard were lifeless and therefore, I expected more of the same. Much to my surprise, there was something different about this teaching. He was quoting scriptures; however, I didn't know that at the time. As a catholic, we were not allowed to read the Bible. That was only meant for the hierarchy.

His teaching drew me like a magnet. It was as if I was drinking a cool, refreshing drink of water in a parched and dry wilderness. That was the best way I could describe this experience. John 6:63 explains it succinctly, ***"It is the Spirit who gives life; the flesh profits nothing. The words I speak to you they are spirit, and they are life."***

I was now feeling that life Jesus had described. I left this meeting feeling refreshed, however, it wasn't enough for me to want to go back. I was too much of a traditional catholic to want change. There were happenings at this meeting that left me confused and baffled, such as praying out loud, raising hands and shouting hallelujah. I didn't understand any of this and I felt out of place.

Upon our departure, a nun gave me a tract that read, "Why Pray in Tongues." I took it out of respect but had no intention of reading it. I came home and flung it on the counter. Two weeks later as we had just moved, I went into my little boy's room to finish unpacking. As

I was sweeping under his bed, this tract came flying out. It seemed that the Holy Spirit wasn't through with me. The tract was like a magnet drawing me. I began reading it and suddenly a strong desire came over me.

It was the same thing I had felt at that meeting two weeks earlier. I know now it was the Holy Spirit drawing me. I wanted what I had just read, and God wanted to give me more of Himself. I needed this peace—this power and abundance of life that was promised.

I got on my knees, and I mimicked what I had seen at the prayer meeting. I raised my hand and began chanting hallelujah. God knew the cries of my heart. He knew exactly what I wanted and what I needed. After a short while, I was overwhelmed with the presence of God and began speaking in a language I had never heard. I experienced a peace I had never felt before.

John 14:27 says, *"Peace I leave with you, My peace I give to you; not as the world gives do I give to you."* Also, in Matthew 5:6 we read, *"Blessed are they who hunger and thirst for righteousness, For they shall be filled."*

Then it happened. I was absolutely filled! That was a holy moment I will never forget, and I haven't been the same since. It was such a miracle because I was so ignorant of God's ways. I didn't know what born-again meant or repentance or anything. However, God knows our hearts. He gave me such a hunger for His Word. I began to voraciously read the Word of God. It was filling a void I had had for years.

Several years later, I was diagnosed with severe scoliosis and could barely walk. I had been outfitted with a cumbersome corset and a platform shoe about an inch high. The orthopedic surgeon had ordered a wheelchair for me and told me I would be in a wheelchair for the rest of my life. Under such overwhelming odds, I couldn't believe that God wanted me to raise my four children from a wheelchair. And, I had never been discipled in biblical truths on healing.

I got on my knees and asked God if healing was only for the book of Acts and not for the present. The Holy Spirit brought to my remembrance some of the healing scriptures I had read so many times. Proverbs 3:7-8 says, *"Do not wise in your own eyes; fear the LORD and depart from evil. It will be health to your flesh and strength to your bones"* (KJV). I also read in Isaiah 53 that by His stripes I was already healed. I said, "God, if healing is for today because you said, in Hebrews 13:8, that Jesus is the same yesterday, today, and forever, does this apply to me, Lord?"

Yes, it did apply to me. I felt the holy fire of God on my spine, and I knew God had healed me of severe scoliosis. I'm a walking miracle and complete in Him according to Colossians 2:10. I not only received a supernatural miracle in the baptism of the Holy Spirit, but as a result, I also received a physical miracle later. Here I am many years later, a senior citizen, without any sign of scoliosis!

Let's pray: *Oh Father, truly You are the same today as You were in The Book of Acts! Your manifold blessings and gifts are available for Your followers just as they were back then. We are so grateful. Help us to surrender to You and lift our hands and our hearts to receive all You desire for each one of us. In Jesus' name we pray, amen.*

Have you experienced the fullness of the Holy Spirit in any way similar to Verna's experience? Have you received a miraculous healing? Tell us your story or your desire, using the hashtag, #HolyGroundAndMe

Power from on High
(Pentecost – New Testament)

Wait in Jerusalem for the ***Promise of the Father*** was Jesus' instruction to His disciples. He had risen to life from death but needed to go away for a little while. He explained, ***"for John truly baptized with water, but you shall be baptized with the Holy Spirit not many days from now"*** (Acts 1:4).

"But you shall receive power when the Holy Spirit has come upon you; and you shall be witnesses to Me in Jerusalem, and in all Judea and Samaria, and to the end of the earth" (Acts 1:8).

And then it happened. On the Day of Pentecost, the disciples were gathered in Jerusalem, unified, just as Jesus had instructed.

"And suddenly there came a sound from heaven, as of a rushing mighty wind, and it filled the whole house where they were sitting. Then there appeared to them divided tongues, as of fire, and one sat upon each of them. And they were all filled with the Holy Spirit and began to speak with other tongues, as the Spirit gave them utterance" (Acts 2:1-4).

As always, God's timing is impeccable. Because of the festival of Passover, also known as the Feast of Weeks and the Day of Firstfruits, thousands of Jews were in the city to celebrate.

The sounds captured their attention and according to Acts 2:6 a multitude gathered around to see what was going on. As they assembled, the disciples poured out into the streets proclaiming the Good News of Jesus Christ. What a holy moment it was!

By His Spirit, God empowered the disciples to speak in the various languages of those people. Acts 2:9-11 lists many of the areas and countries represented there who were hearing, for the first time, ***"the wonderful works of God"*** (v.11b).

Some attendees thought the disciples were drunk.

"But Peter, standing up with the eleven, raised his voice and said to them, 'Men if Judea and all who dwell in Jerusalem, let this be known to you, and heed my words. For these are not drunk as you suppose, since it is only the third hour of the day. But this is

what was spoken by the prophet Joel" (Acts 2:14-16).

Then, for the next few verses we read Peter quoting some of Joel's prophesies and preaching a powerful sermon. He also included psalms of David proclaiming the coming Messiah.

What happened next was amazing. The world became a whole new place for many of those people who were standing on the holy ground of the streets of Jerusalem.

Peter urged them to *"Be saved from this perverse generation"* (Acts 2:40b).

"Then those who gladly received his word were baptized; and that day about three thousand souls were added to them" (Acts 2:41).

The disciples continued on in the power of the Holy Spirit. Plus, God was giving that same power to others through the Baptism of the Holy Spirit as we see in many instances throughout the rest of the New Testament. And it's wonderful that the Gift of Tongues, along with the other eight spiritual gifts are available to God's people even to this day.

Back there in first Century Acts the Church of Jesus Christ exploded. People groups from all over the known world were hearing and receiving the Salvation of the Gospel. The world was changed because so many people were changed.

Are you praying for revival—an explosion of the scattering of the Good News to spread across our land and the world? I certainly am.

Referring to Acts 2:40-47, Dr. Ryan Jackson* said that this is "what a church of increase looks like—theologically deep and evangelically wide." Let's be this church, both within the walls of our buildings and out in the marketplace of our daily lives.

We should be praying for lost souls—that the world may know of Jesus and His great Salvation. That is the commissioning of every follower of Jesus Christ—praying and proclaiming.

Let's pray: *Holy God, thank You for sending the "Promise of the Father" to endue us with power to do the work You have called us to do. Help each of us to receive with joy all You have for us and to be Your people in this hour proclaiming Your Good News so that multitudes will be saved. In Jesus' name we pray, Amen.*

Have you heard about the Baptism in the Holy Spirit spoken of in Acts 2? Have you experienced, for yourself, this Baptism in the Holy Spirit? Feel free to share your own experience using the hashtag, #HolyGroundAndMe

*Dr. Ryan Jackson is the Senior Pastor of The Capital Church, Garner, North Carolina

My Life Changing Supernatural Encounter
(Diana Lookabaugh)

When my cousin asked me to write about a supernatural life changing encounter with God I'd had for her book, I knew exactly what it had to be!

It began when several friends in Thomasville, Georgia shared an amazing experience with me. It took a year for me to search it out for myself but once I saw and understood how scriptural and important this experience was for a vibrant, victorious Christian life, I embraced it and Jesus with all my heart, and I received it!

Along with the Bible, several books that helped in my quest are: *The Cross and the Switchblade*, by David Wilkerson, *Beyond Our Selves*, and *Something More* by Catherine Marshall, and *A New Song*, by Pat Boone along with many more books with powerful testimonies of how God was impacting many lives.

Somewhere I read, *"Read your Bible and underline every time you see 'Holy Spirit.'"*

So, I did just that and became convinced this spiritual gift was and is from God to equip all believers who will receive it. What is this Gift? It is the precious Baptism in the Holy Spirt!

John the Baptist said Jesus is the one who will baptize you with the Holy Spirt and Fire. Upon His departure, Jesus told his disciples to wait in Jerusalem until they had received the Holy Spirit and power to be his witnesses.

"And being assembled together with them, He (Jesus) ***commanded them not to depart from Jerusalem but to wait for the Promise of the Father, which, He said, 'you have heard from Me; for John truly baptized with water, but you shall be baptized with the Holy Spirit not many days from now"*** (Acts 1:4-5).

Please recall and re-read Acts 2 and the Day of Pentecost to see this for yourself. A rushing mighty wind, tongues of fire on each one there, and they all spoke in tongues in another language. Keep reading!

Somehow this important and powerful Baptism in the Spirit had gotten lost or overlooked and neglected in my Christian upbringing, but suddenly a fresh Baptism of the Holy Spirit was being poured out in all denominations and I was fortunate and blessed to receive it also!

After receiving prayer by my friends, I knelt by my bed and asked Jesus to come into my heart, forgive me of my sins, and take over my life from then on. I also asked Jesus to baptize me with the Holy Spirit with evidence like they had at Pentecost.

Then it happened! I was born again and Baptized in the Spirit and began singing in another language with tears of joy running down my cheeks. It was real! I was on holy ground right there in my bedroom!

This experience with Jesus changed my life forever. I have never been the same nor would I ever want to be without this supernatural power to live the Christian life and be His witness. It's been fifty-three years now in a closer walk with Jesus, empowered by Holy Spirit.

I've seen many miracles of healing in my own family and elsewhere. One that stands out was in 1973, while my mother was visiting us in Thomasville, Georgia. We rode on a chartered bus with Spirit-filled Episcopalians to attend a Kathryn Kuhlman meeting in Jacksonville, Florida.

Many wonderful miracles took place that day in Miss Kuhlman's crusade, but we never dreamed my mother would receive one of them! I didn't even know she'd been diagnosed in 1972 with a terminal blood disorder!

Mother and I left filled with faith after witnessing and hearing testimonies of many who were healed that day.

When Mother got back to her home in Radford, Virginia where I grew up, her doctor was amazed to find her totally healed of the terminal blood disease. "Frances, you are a walking miracle!" he said. And she was! God extended her life 15 more years to see all eight of her grandchildren.

It's been thrilling to experience many of the Nine Gifts of Holy Spirit listed in 1 Corinthians 12, which are all real for today. And I want to display all the Nine Fruits of Holy Spirit listed in Galatians 5:22. They are Love, Joy, Peace, Patience, Kindness, Goodness, Faithfulness, Gentleness and Self Control.

This all happened to me in 1971 while living in Thomasville, GA. It was like *living* the Book of Acts! And still is.

Those of us who had been baptized in Holy Spirit met often to worship and pray. We devoured the Bible and numerous books and cassette tapes with testimonies of other believers.

The Lord had me start a luncheon meeting at a prominent Woman's Club Building in Thomasville where women of all denominations attended and heard Spirit-filled speakers. It was very exciting!

Then in 1977 my husband was transferred to Denton, Tx. and a new adventure began! My calling to gather, nurture and raise up women in the faith continued when I was asked to lead Denton Women's Aglow for six years, then plowed ground at Texas Woman's University and beyond.

Then fifteen years ago Apostle Chuck Pierce asked me to start Women's House of Zion under Glory of Zion International. We're still going strong and multiplying. These women's groups enjoy Worship, Word, Ministry and Fellowship under gifted leaders in homes and via Zoom. In September we expect to have 70 or more strong Houses in 15 states, Finland, and the Bahamas!

It is rewarding to oversee these Houses and to see all that God is doing in each one! You can find us at Gloryofzion.org to inquire and join one. We also have a FB page: Women's Houses of Zion with inspirational posts.

Thank you, Connie, for this opportunity to share!

Diana Cox Lookabaugh

dianalook@aol.com

Let's pray: *Holy Father, how can we ever thank You enough for all you do for us? Not only have You removed our sins by way of the shed blood of Your dear Son, Jesus, but You have given us power from on High. You have granted us the mighty Gift of Your own Holy Spirit through baptizing us with immersion in that very Spirit. Thank You Lord, for ALL that comes with this wonderful Gift, helping your*

Have you been Baptized in the Holy Spirit and would like to share your experience? How did it affect you? Feel free to share your experience using the hashtag, #HolyGroundAndMe

A Second Touch
(Ephesians, Baptized Again - New Testament)

I love it when Scripture says, ***"And it happened."*** That's the way the nineteenth chapter of Acts begins.

On his third missionary journey, Paul returned to Ephesus, just as he had promised. Encountering a group of believers, ***"he said to them, 'Did you receive the Holy Spirit when you believed?' So, they said to him 'We have not so much as heard whether there is a Holy Spirit.'***

"And he said to them, 'Into what then were you baptized?' So they said, 'Into John's baptism.' Then Paul said, 'John indeed baptized with a baptism of repentance, saying to the people that they should believe on Him who would come after him, that is Christ Jesus.'" (Acts 19:2-4).

Upon believing Paul's explanation, they were baptized in the name of the Lord Jesus. Interestingly, this is the only mention in Scripture of anyone being water baptized a second time.

"And when Paul had laid hands on them, the Holy Spirit came upon them, and they spoke with tongues and prophesied" (Acts 19:6).

These men had not only come into faith in Jesus but into another dimension of spirituality. Unaware of the upper room Pentecostal occurrence they didn't know there existed a fuller spiritual experience. They didn't know that the promised power from on high had come to earth. Scripture tells of other instances in which people received Jesus' promised baptism with the Holy Spirit, (Acts 1:5), with the evidence of speaking in tongues in Acts 2:24 and in Acts 10:44-46.

The spiritual gift of speaking in tongues is not a requirement for being born-again and, yes, we automatically receive the indwelling Holy Spirit in the moment when we believe and receive Christ as our Lord and Savior. But when the holy moment of Holy Spirit Baptism occurs in a believer, the usual results include increased hunger for God's Word, greater desire and boldness to spread the Gospel, increased inner joy, and undeniable assurance of one's personal salvation. Also, not uncommon is the enduement of one or more of the nine spiritual gifts listed in 1 Corinthians 12:8-10. They include word of wisdom, word of knowledge, faith, gifts of healing, the working of miracles, prophecy, the discerning of spirits, different kinds of tongues, and the interpretation of tongues.

Many Christians are unaware of the reality of this second touch of the Holy Spirit, and some believe it's not for today though the Bible never says such a thing. If you have not received this gift and would like to do so, study and meditate in the Book of Acts and underline everywhere you see the words "Holy Spirit." Talk with God about it and be open to receive. If you have experienced it, ask God to help you use and enjoy your gift fully.

Let's pray: *Holy Father, You are the giver of wonderful gifts for our personal edification and for the edification of Your body. Thank You. Help me receive all that You have for me so I can be more of what You want and more effective for service in the building of Your Kingdom. In Jesus' name, amen.*

Please share your Holy Spirit gift experience or desire for it using the hashtag, #HolyGroundAndMe

God is Good
(Gary H.)

He was hit in the head by a moose … right in his own yard! It wasn't just any moose though. Gary tells it like this:

April 3, 2020, was like any other Friday, or so it seemed. I was in my garage painting a big moose that I had cut out of wood. Upon finishing, I carried it outside to dry in the sun. Walking backwards with it I stepped off the edge of my driveway and fell back.

I fell in the grass and the moose fell and hit me on the head. I called my older daughter and let her know that I had taken a spill and filled her in on the details. I don't remember much that happened the rest of the day.

The next day I awakened with a head that was really hurting. Again, I called my daughter, and she scheduled an appointment for me to see a doctor. Sometime after lunch that day I got into my car and took off. I don't know where I went. I thought I was going to my brother's house in a neighboring community, but he later told me that I did not stop at his place that day.

Sometime later, I was stopped at a red light, and sat there as the light changed three times. A Sherriff's deputy was sitting behind me and finally blew his horn to encourage me to move. I took off, changed lanes, and even went through another light and pulled over at a parking lot down the road, followed by the deputy.

The deputy got me out of the car and made me take a breathalyzer test. I blew a .00, probably to his surprise. At that same time my brother pulled in to see what was going on. The deputy had me away from the car attempting to walk in a straight line. Unsurprisingly, I was unable to do that or any other tasks he asked me to complete. The deputy advised my brother that I was likely having a medical episode, and my brother informed him I was supposed to be in a doctor's appointment at that time.

My brother drove me to the local CVS to see a doctor, the original site of my medical appointment. When we got there both of my daughters were waiting for me, even though I barely recall them at all. One of them called 911 and an ambulance soon arrived to take me for more observations.

I remember praying to God, asking Him to take care of my daughters. I told Him that my life was in His hands and that I was ready for the next journey. I don't remember arriving at the hospital in Radford and they subsequently transported me to a higher-level hospital in Roanoke, Virginia.

I learned later that someone called my daughter from Roanoke and stated that they were going to put me on a respirator. They didn't think I was dying, but that I did need help breathing. I stayed on that machine for a week.

It's hard to imagine what my family was going through at the time. All they could do was call into the hospital and ask for updates. This was during the period of time when, because of the pandemic, family members were not allowed to visit loved ones who were hospitalized.

As it turned out, the diagnosis did not sound very appealing. Doctors thought it might be anything from a mini stroke, to a heart attack, to kidney failure, or something else. My daughters were told that even if I survived, I would likely be on medications such as dialysis to keep me going. Things looked grim.

Then it happened. Somewhere in that time frame, my life changed. I vividly recall that I was lying on a flat, steel gurney. I was in a dimly lit room with a sign on the wall that read, "afterlife." I thought to myself that I must be dead. A little man was standing beside me with something in his hand and started rubbing me up and down. I asked him what he was doing, and he replied with these words, "Getting you ready for the afterlife."

He asked me if I knew him and I said, "Yes, you are Mike, and we worked together at the foundry." I knew he had died a long time ago.

He walked out of the room and told me he would come back in three minutes. Suddenly, a bright light appeared at my feet. All I could see was a figure dressed in a white cloth with his hands crossed. He stated, "He is going with me."

Once I heard that voice, I completely relaxed, crossed my hands on my chest and took relief in the fact that I knew where my journey was taking me. I knew that God's glorious light was shining on me, and God's mighty voice spoke calmly to me. I felt a peace that I had never previously felt. I was on holy ground in a holy moment like none I'd ever encountered before.

Then I was in recovery for a couple of days. I was lying in bed when my eyes opened to see a man dressed in a white coat and mask asking me how I was doing. I let him know that I was feeling great, and I knew nothing about the last seven days except for the fact that God was in control.

He proceeded with a few tests and told others in the room that he thought I was going to be all right. A few days later I walked out of the hospital feeling like a brand-new man. The story doesn't end here though.

We cannot forget about the power of prayer. I learned later just how many people were praying for me, but one account stood out in particular. A lady from my church was having a phone conversation with me after I got home and told me she was praying doubly hard for me one morning. She saw me laying at the foot of a bright light and God let her see that He was with me. I will never forget that.

In all of this, I'm reminded of the cross. I know that God has a plan for each one of us. A lot of things that I did in my life were not right in His eyes, but I did know that what I did was taken care of on the cross. The cross means something to me. It was on a wooden cross that Jesus Christ died to take the punishment that I deserved and I'm forever grateful.

John 14:6 tells us the way to receive this redemption. ***"Jesus said to him, 'I am the way, the truth, and the life. No one comes to the Father except through Me.'"***

A little cross was with me for my whole tour in Vietnam. You might be familiar with the small crosses that are sometimes given along with a card with a poem titled "The Cross in My Pocket." It is one of those. I gave my cross to other soldiers before being deployed overseas and they returned it to me upon their arrival home. They too know the power of prayer.

I made a fairly large wooden cross which now stands in my yard. Ride by my house, day or night, and you will see my cross.

I have learned to know that I serve an awesome God. God is good—all the time.

Let's pray: *Oh, God, yes You are good! Yes, You are good all the time. Thank You for the privilege of prayer and that You turn Your ear to hear our pleas. Lord, what a precious thing that You visited Gary, giving him assurance that You could see his situation and had him in Your capable hands. You gave him peace and calm in the midst of his dire condition. Thank You for the cross and the precious blood that Your Son shed for the remission of our sins. Oh, Father, we're so grateful. Help us to live for You and share your love and greatness with others along our way. In Jesus' name we pray, amen.*

If you have encountered a visitation from God or one of His angels, please share your experience using the hashtag, #HolyGroundAndMe

[Side Note: (Connie here.) When Gary was so ill in the hospital, I stayed in touch with his daughter regarding his condition and continued to pray for him. When I realized that his condition was grave, I turned up the heat on my prayers, praying fervently for his recovery. I was heartbroken that his daughters were not allowed to visit him in the hospital, so I asked God to visit him or send an angel to visit him and give him divine peace. God assured me and showed me that He was doing just that. After that, I looked forward to talking with Gary and hearing all about it and don't you know that I was thrilled to hear his testimony. Yes, indeed, our God is awesome, and He is oh so good, all the time!]

This Same Jesus
(Jesus' Ascension - New Testament)

The recent days and weeks had been ablaze with emotion—exhausting, sorrowful, confusing, shame-filled, exhilarating, relief-filled, and now anticipatory. Followers of Jesus had experienced them all.

Their Friend and Teacher had been falsely accused, was crucified, had died, was buried, and then gloriously raised from the dead. Then, for several days, He appeared to many people. It was no secret that Jesus, who they had watched die on a cross, was now very much alive.

His disciples gathered with their risen Lord and He gave encouragement and instructions on what to do next as they waited for the Promise of the Father. Then on Mount Olivet a most astounding thing happened. Jesus was taken up into the sky in a cloud. He had told them He would be leaving and that they would receive the Baptism in the Holy Spirit to be endued with God's power. They had no idea His departure would play out in such a dramatic manner.

So now in this moment, He was gone.

"And while they looked steadfastly toward heaven as He went up, behold, two men stood by them in white apparel, who also said, 'Men of Galilee, why do you stand gazing up into heaven? This same Jesus, who was taken up from you into heaven, will so come in like manner as you saw Him go into heaven'" (Acts 1:10-11).

In that holy moment on the holy ground of the Mount of Olives, Jesus' disciples watched as He was lifted up and disappeared. What did they think? How did they feel? How long did they stand there and stare at the sky?

Do you ever gaze at the sky and anticipate Jesus' return? I do.

He is coming back. We don't know the day nor the hour, but we're instructed to watch and pray and anticipate. We must ready ourselves and do the work of His Kingdom until He returns. Luke records the Parable of the Minas in which the nobleman, who was going away, told his servants to ***"Do business till I come"*** (Luke 19:13b). The King James Version says, ***"Occupy till I come."***

So, that's what we're to be doing now—doing the things Jesus taught His followers to do. His teachings are recorded in the four Gospels: Matthew, Mark, Luke, and John, plus in the Book of Acts. All the other New Testament books are instructive and give many examples of how to live for Christ and fulfill The Great Commission. So, what is The Great Commission?

The Great Commission is recorded in the book of Matthew when Jesus instructed his followers: ***"Go ye therefore, and teach all nations, baptizing them in the name of the Father, and of the Son, and of the Holy Ghost: teaching them to observe all things whatsoever I have commanded you: and, lo, I am with you always, even unto the end of the world. Amen"*** (Matthew 28:19-20 KJV).

Sadly, many Christians and self-proclaimed-but-not-real Christians do not read and study their Bibles. Therefore, how can they know how to do the work of God's Kingdom? Plus, they may not realize that God's abundant life for them personally is passing them by. Instead, their apathy toward God's Word is allowing the devil to rob them of their best life. Jesus said, ***"The thief comes only to steal and kill and destroy; I came that they may have life, and have it abundantly"*** (John 10:10 NASB).

When we gaze at the sky let's anticipate and be grateful. We have been given everything we need to live successfully for Christ. We have His instructions and examples in His Book and we have access to His power through His Spirit.

Let's pray: *Holy Father, thank You for Jesus. Thank You for giving us His power. Yes, I believe in Jesus—that He is Your own Son who took the punishment I deserved for my own sins. Help me, Lord, to do the work of Your Kingdom on earth. I look to You and to Your Word to show me the way to daily walk out my time on earth while I continue to look up for Your glorious return. In Jesus' name I pray, amen.*

Are you looking up? Have you ever seen clouds shaped like angels or something that caused you to be in awe of your Creator? (Maybe those clouds really are angels.) What are you doing to help you occupy till He comes? Please share your experiences and thoughts using the hashtag, #HolyGroundAndMe

[Side Note: (Connie here.) Speaking of Jesus' return, I had a rather interesting experience on May 21, 2011. That was the date which a Christian radio host had predicted would be the day of the Rapture and Judgement Day. Well, as it happened, I was in Israel at the time. On the morning of May 21 our tour group gathered on the Mount of Olives for our morning teaching and tour experience. We were all rather amused to be right there on the spot where Jesus will return on what the Bible often refers to as "that day." As expected, He did not come back on that day while we were there. Plus, the mountain did not split in two from east to west as prophesied in Zachariah 14:4. Along with our leader/teacher, Joel Rosenberg, we all looked at the sky above the Holy City and saw no sign of our returning King.

I've never understood why people make such predictions when the Bible clearly states that no one will know the day nor the hour. But we can be sure He will return, and it will be the most wonderfully amazing experience of a lifetime for those of us who are in Christ Jesus and are still hanging out in our earthly bodies.]

HOLY, HOLY, HOLY
(Throne Room of God)

"I was in the Spirit on the Lord's Day" (Revelation 1:10a), John says as he begins to describe the vision the Lord imparts to him—and the earth began to quake and tremble.

Moving on to Chapter 4 he sees a door standing open and the throne room of Heaven is in view. Like the sound of a trumpet a voice thunders, ***"Come up here, and I will show you things which must take place after this"*** (Revelation 4:1b).

In the next few verses John describes God, His throne, and its surroundings. He sees precious stones as he explains God Himself, surrounded by a rainbow. Also, around Him are twenty-four elders clad in white linen, each one on a throne and wearing a crown of gold. These are believed to be the twelve apostles and the twelve sons of Israel (Jacob).

John sees many things, hard to explain in human terms—lightenings, thundering voices, lamps of fire, and the sea of glass like crystal. Around the throne are four living creatures with many eyes, each with six wings and other unique features. ***"And they do not rest day or night, saying: 'Holy, holy, holy, Lord God Almighty, who was and is and is to come!'"*** (Revelation 4:8b).

The apostle, John, has surely been placed on holy ground and is witnessing the most holy place of all time in all the universe and beyond. The holiness of Yahweh is being revealed to him as he's given a glimpse of the glorious future awaiting those of us who are in Christ Jesus.

When God or Jesus repeats a word or phrase twice it is for emphasis. Here God is described as "holy, holy, holy." Using the word holy three times depicts extreme emphasis. Plus, it is repeated over and over by the creatures. Also, when it was stated, the elders cast their crowns before the throne and proclaim, ***"You are worthy, O Lord, to receive glory and honor and power"*** (Revelation 4:11b).

The prophet Isaiah had a vision seeing seraphim standing near God's throne. One of them cried out, ***"Holy, holy, holy, is the LORD of hosts: the whole earth is full of His glory"*** (Isaiah 6:3b).

The holiness of God is beyond our imaginations as human beings. The highest degree of superlative descriptive words in any language on the planet cannot come close to expressing how holy—how magnificent—how powerful is our God.

But one day we will know. We will understand. For now, we see through a glass dimly. (1 Corinthians 13:12). Those of us who are born-again followers of Christ Jesus will indeed experience, in person, in our glorified perfect bodies the holy, holy, holiness of God and King Jesus. We will each be given a crown which we will joyfully cast before the throne of God. For each of us, what a glorious day that will certainly be!

Let's pray: *Oh, holy Father, indeed Your holiness, Your majesty, Your power, and Your awesomeness is beyond what we can imagine. But You have made a way, through the blood of Your dear Son, for us to dwell in Your presence forever. You have prepared a heavenly home for us. All You ask for in return is ourselves. You ask that we give You our whole selves—our lives—our wills—our griefs and sorrows—our burdens and cares—our pasts—our futures—our sins—everything that we are and have. In the Great Exchange You give us everything You are and have—love unfailing, peace, joy, hope, and much more. Thank You, Abba Father. In our gratitude, help us to live for you and walk in Your ways. In Jesus' name, amen.*

Have you experienced a vision of God? Have you heard Him speak to you in a thundering voice or in a still small voice? Many years ago, I had a very brief glimpse of God on His throne, but I have never heard the audible voice of God ... yet. Please share your experience or comment using the hashtag #HolyGroundAndMe

Epilogue

In conclusion, I pray that the testimonies in this little book serve to encourage people and build faith. In no way should these stories cause a person to feel they've been left out or overlooked when God is giving out gifts, blessings, or miracles. He does not esteem one person higher than another for we are each created by God in His own image. (Genesis 1:27).

When one wishes to receive blessings from God, I recommend doing these things: honor and fear God in all your ways; learn Jesus and His ways by systematic reading, studying, and meditating on Scripture; pray a lot every day, talking to Father God as a beloved Daddy and Friend; sit quietly before the Lord listening and marveling at how awesome He is; tell God what you desire whether it's healing, financial help, a spiritual gift, friendship, or whatever is on your heart. Be assured you will not hurt God's feelings nor make Him mad no matter what you say to Him. He completely understands every thought we think and motive we have and continues to love each one of us unconditionally with unfailing love.

Love is key for God is love (1 John 4:16). When Jesus was asked what the greatest Commandment is, He said, "The first of all the commandments is: 'Hear, O Israel, the LORD our God, the LORD is one. And you shall love the LORD your God with all your heart, with all your soul, with all your mind, and with all your strength.' This is the first commandment. And the second, like it, is this: 'You shall love your neighbor as yourself.' There is no other commandment greater than these" (Mark 12:29-31).

Doing the things mentioned above honor God, plus I want to add another important thing. Believe Jesus and believe in Jesus. "But without faith it is impossible to please Him, for he who comes to God must believe that He is, and that He is a rewarder of those who diligently seek Him" (Hebrews 11:6).

Thank you for reading Holy Ground: Have You Been There?. May the grace of Jesus be with you always and may His blessings overtake you. Connie

#HolyGroundAndMe

More Books by Connie Wohlford

Pocket Inspirational Books

Loving Children: Praying
God's Word Over Them

I Declare God's
Word Is True

Children's Books

Joy Comes To
Bethlehem

His Name Is
Jesus

He Is
The One

The Lord Has
Need Of You

You're A What?

Make It A
Happy Day

For additional information contact Connie via email: wohlfordconnie@gmail.com

Connect on Facebook: https://www.facebook.com/ConnieWohlfordAuthor

Blog: www.GodsWordOurDestiny.wordpress.com

Cash, check, credit card <> Sales Tax in Virginia. Nominal fee for shipping.

All of Connie's books are proudly 100% Made in U.S.A.